CHARACTERS
WITH
CHARACTER

CHARACTERS
WITH
CHARACTER
SERMONS on SAINTS
DAVID M. GRIFFIS

Pathway
PRESS

Unless noted, all Scripture quotations are from the King James Version of the Bible.

Library of Congress Catalog Card Number: 99-64897

ISBN: 0-87148-211-8

Dedication

To my Dad, the Reverend Garland M. Griffis,

A scholar, teacher and preacher of God's Word.

His character enables him to live what he preaches,

So that his children "rise up and call him
blessed."

CONTENTS

ACKNOWLEDGEMENTS

I want to thank the many people who have assisted me and have lended valuable advice in this project.

Marcus Hand, outstanding Christian writer and my editor, did a masterful job with the manuscript.

Bill George, editor in chief for Pathway Press, encouraged me from the very beginning to see the project through.

My good friend, *Dan Boling*, director of publications, gave his whole-hearted endorsement for the book's publication.

Wayne Slocumb, one of the best in the business, did a masterful job on the cover design.

My personal secretary, *Joyce Guiles*, typed and retyped the manuscript with patience and expertise.

And most of all, to the *holy men of God* who were moved by the Holy Spirit (2 Peter 1:20, 21) to write the 66 books of the Bible from whence these marvelous characters emerged—to them I say, "Thank you!"

FOREWORD

In a day of relative morality and autonomous ethics, it is imperative that we as Christians explore the true meaning of "Christian character."

As David Griffis reviews the great saints of the Bible, we learn how to function in the modern world through their commitment to absolute principles of Biblical truth embodied in a personal experience with God.

This is one of those books that is a "must" for every born-again believer in every walk of life.

Drawing from his vast experience in ministry and Christian education in local churches, author Griffis presents the problems confronted in everyday circumstances and offers solutions for victorious living.

As a denominational leader, I have observed the ministry of David Griffis through the years, and in this resource he shares his heart for God and his dedication to help Christian leaders alike in being more effective and efficient in Kingdom outreach.

I whole-heartedly recommend *Characters With Character: Sermons on Saints* as an important tool to help equip those in the outreach of Christian ministry and the continuing development of spiritual living.

— *Paul L. Walker*, Ph.D.
General Overseer, Church of God

INTRODUCTION

THE 66 BOOKS THAT COMPRISE HOLY SCRIPTURE contain the true wisdom of the ages. Within their pages, we find the Word and will of Almighty God. But God has also chosen the fleshly lives of men and women in which to reveal His great truths to us.

We know that angels bring messages from the throne, and that Christ conveys the will of the Father to us in His Deity. Through temples of clay, God continues to manifest Himself. Brilliantly and consistently, the lives of Biblical characters reflect God's love for us and His expectations of us.

This book is written to explore and define both Old and New Testament saints; and to paint portraits of their lives through expository language. Although dead for millennia (with the noted exception of Enoch), they speak loudly through the centuries.

Together their lives comprise a mosaic of the human experience. Their strengths are our strengths; their weaknesses, our weaknesses. They are not flawless, yet their frailties were often springboards for triumph.

The single factor they have in common is their resolute faith in God. Although they all were sorely tested, and sometimes their humanity was stretched to the maximum, they endured and saw the glory of victory.

Come with me and see the red blood of Abel stain the early earth. Marvel at the tenacity of an 80-year-old

Caleb bursting out of a wilderness to fight giants and armies of renown.

Look with me at Job, a wasted, emaciated, diseased human whose body has shriveled to skin-over-skeleton, and hear him proclaim, "Though He slay me, yet will I trust Him" (Job 13:15).

Feel the excitement of the ancient prophet who lifts his doddering head and is filled with power as an 8-day-old baby is brought to the temple for circumcision. Sense what Simeon saw when He knew, beyond a doubt, that this baby was *the* Baby.

Image if you will, the feeling of wonder and fear in the heart of a teenage Hebrew girl, in a tiny mountainous village, as she stands before God's mighty messenger angel, Gabriel, and hears for the first time that she will be the mother of the Messiah.

No wonder, the Bible is still the greatest book ever written. These stories will be told as long as the human voice can speak.

Join me in the excitement of learning again these lessons from holy men and women. May these sermons on saints be a mirror that enables us to examine ourselves; and in so doing may we too become better men and women.

May we too be saints of God!

– David Griffis

PART I

Saints of the Old Testament

Time would fail me to tell of . . . others . . . . (Of
whom the world was not worthy). . . . And these
all . . . obtained a good report through faith
(Hebrews 11:32, 36, 38, 39).

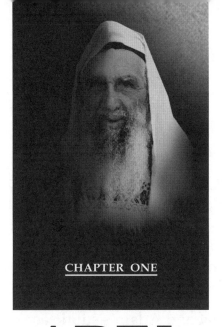

CHAPTER ONE

ABEL
The Voice From Beyond the Grave

And the Lord had respect unto Abel and to his offering
(Genesis 4:4).

ALTHOUGH HIS TIME ON EARTH WAS SHORT, Abel distinguished his life in many ways. According to the scriptural record, Abel was the first man to die.

The curse of death was pronounced on the human race through his mother and father in a forest glade of Eden's garden. The divine Judge Himself handed down the capital sentence.

But who could have foreseen the fact that the supreme penalty would be visited first on the child of Adam and Eve, the guilty couple?

Not only would death come to Adam's family, but it would manifest itself first in the foul and heinous reality of murder. Further, this murder would happen in vicious rage and the perpetrator would be none other than the unfortunate victim's own brother.

Eve's belief and Adam's subtle acceptance of the serpent's lie beneath the canopy of Eden's beauty begins to reap horrible consequences.

The only redeeming concept in the story of this first family is the godly character of the murder victim, Abel.

ABEL'S GODLY CHARACTER

Genesis 4:1, 2 tells of the conception and birth of the brothers, Cain and Abel. Since conception is mentioned only once (v. 1), many scholars believe that Cain and Abel may have been twins. Nevertheless, they were brothers and grew up together in the humanity's earliest days on earth.

Their interests were totally different, for Cain was "a tiller of the ground" and Abel was a "keeper of the sheep" (v. 2). Cain planted crops and kept vineyards while his brother, Abel, was a herdsman.

God's Sheep Keepers

The Hebrew language of Genesis 4:2 says that Abel was a *feeder* of the flocks, denoting his total care of those living creatures.

Many great men in Scripture "kept" the flocks.

✓ Abraham took his flocks from Ur to the land of Canaan (Genesis 12:16).

✓ Moses was tending sheep in the wilderness of Midian when he saw the bush that burned but was not consumed (see Exodus 3:1, 2).

✓ David, the sweet psalmist of Israel and the greatest of her kings, was first a shepherd (1 Samuel 16:11).

✓ Amos, the prophet, was a herdsman (Amos 7:14).

✓ Jesus called Himself "the good shepherd" (John 10:14).

✓ Indeed, lowly shepherds were the first to sojourn into Bethlehem to worship the infant Messiah (see Luke 2:15, 16).

None of this makes a shepherd more pleasing to the Lord than one who labors in any other occupation. However, we see certain character qualities that must be present to make one a successful shepherd.

Jesus himself made us aware of those characteristics. A shepherd has the trusting heart of the sheep for he has never harmed them, but has always benefitted them by his actions.

In John 10:1-10, Jesus used the illustration of the shepherd who kept his sheep in a corral with only one door. The shepherd would sleep in the doorway. To get to the sheep, a predator or thief would have to go over the shepherd.

Jesus reminded us that the shepherd literally places his life on the line for his sheep. Jesus said the thief comes "to steal, and to kill, and to destroy" (John 10:10). A thief butchers the sheep and sells the mutton and wool.

A good shepherd gives the sheep life and provides the best for them. Sheep know the voice of their shepherd and follow only him, for it is the voice of provision and loving care (see vv. 4, 5).

Some may have the occupation of "sheep keepers," but only a true shepherd will give his life for his sheep (see v. 11).

Jesus called the hired sheep-keepers "hirelings." He said that the hireling flees when wolves, predators and thieves come, for one simple reason: "He . . . careth not for the sheep" (John 10:13). This is repeated over and over in the religious world.

Through Christ's example in John 10, Scripture uses the shepherd as a symbolic portrait of what a caring pastor should be. A pastor must have the heart of a true shepherd, and the howl of the wolf must not frighten him away.

He does not watch the flock with monetary gain in mind, but a love for his sheep is his motive. He will not exploit them or despise them. He will sleep in front of the corral door to guard his flock, and if need be, will risk his life for even one lost sheep.

Abel's Excellent Sacrifice

Abel possessed these same characteristics and when it came time for a sacrifice unto the Lord, he took "the firstlings of his flock and of the fat thereof" (Genesis 4:4). This offering consisted of the first offspring of the very flock to which he gave tender care.

He had watched their birth with the love of a shepherd's heart. He remembered their first feeble attempts to stand on little trembling, wooly legs. He watched them run and play and skip across meadows as only young fauna can do. They grew and fattened and became prime specimens of the flock.

Thus, they represented the best he had—and only the best was good enough for the Lord he loved.

Some speculate that God had respect for Abel's sacrifice above Cain's because Abel's sacrifice was one of blood. But the Old Testament is replete with examples of God accepting other sacrifices. Both meat and meal offerings were given to God and accepted under the Mosaic Law.

In fact, the feast of Pentecost was a feast of the first fruits and commemorated the giving of the Law to Moses on Mt. Sinai.

The reason God respected Abel's offering and not Cain's was that Abel's offering was offered in faith (see Hebrews 11:4). Abel gave his very best in love and devotion to God; and his offering was not begrudged.

There is some indication in God's rebuke to Cain that the murderous brother's offering was begrudged (see Genesis 4:7). Hebrews 11:4 calls Abel's gift "a more excellent sacrifice."

Why is this so? Does it refer to a monetary value? Hardly.

Jesus told the story of the little widow in the temple who gave "two mites" (see Luke 21:2, 3). His commentary on her gift, though it was less than a half cent, was that she had "cast in more than they all."

This was a comparison to men whose bags of gold coins made hefty sounds as they dropped in the collection pan. A gift to God then is not measured in earthly value, for after all, the Recipient made the earth and all that is in it. No, gifts to God are measured in the heart of the giver.

Motive, love, faith and devotion all come into play here. Abel's faith immediately labeled his sacrifice "more excellent" than the others.

Cain's Rejected Offering

Cain's demeanor changed when his sacrifice was not approved. The Bible says "And Cain was very wroth and his countenance fell" (Genesis 4:5).

God, who sees all, gave Cain a stern, yet loving rebuke: "Why is thy countenance fallen? If thou doest well, shalt thou not be accepted? And if thou doest not well, sin lieth at the door" (vv. 6, 7).

Cain's anger seethed, however, like a boiling cauldron of destructive acid. His jealous-ridden heart devised a plan for the physical destruction of his own brother.

The original Hebrew text of verse 8 states that after talking with Abel, Cain said, "Let us go out into the field." This phrase indicates premeditation of the murderous act.

Perhaps the field offered cover for the dastardly deed. Perhaps it was far from the ears of the first parents. It could have been a predetermined place where he had a weapon hidden. A grave could have already been dug near the scene of execution.

All of this is speculation, of course, but one thing is certain: the rage that drove Cain to this foul deed was building by the moment.

CAIN'S UNBRIDLED ANGER

Unrequited anger always affects the thinking process. Since the mind or heart of man is desperately wicked, anger plots its satisfaction. Unbridled anger demands fulfillment and most often culminates in violent acts of desperation.

The sin-diseased mind plots as the serpent of sin entices the potential sinner to fill his cup of wrath with deeds of damnation.

Cain worked the fields. Breaking up unbroken ground is hard work and a steady diet of this labor builds muscles and endurance.

The shepherd basically walks and watches. Jacob, the son of Isaac and Rebekah was a shepherd and the Bible indicated his skin and muscle tone was soft (see Genesis 28:16-23).

The strong, burly Cain, in a killing field he had chosen, rose up and slew his brother Abel. Here he buried his slain sibling and casually went back to work—just as if nothing at all had taken place. But God knew better.

The voice of the faithful can never be silenced. Words and admonitions from saints and sages long gone from the earth still guide our world when we heed them.

Death could not still the witnessing voice of godly Abel. His blood-soaked grave was, and is, a pulpit of righteousness crying out to God. The Lord heard the cry of His righteous shepherd.

Cain was judged for his horrible sin. But the judgement of Cain is not the central message of Genesis 4. The writer of the Book of Hebrews says in 11:4 that Abel, whose voice comes from the grave, preaches a six-fold message:

1. Only by faith can you and I truly give anything to God.
2. Only by faith can we give a gift that is accepted as excellent.
3. Only by faith can we be deemed a true witness for God.
4. Only by faith can we be righteous before God.
5. Only by faith can our gifts be accepted by God.

6. Only by faith does our testimony live after our death.

ABEL'S ABIDING TESTIMONY

The message of Abel is still alive. Although this first man to die has long been with the Lord, the passing of centuries has not dulled or lessened his message.

Gifts to God must come from the heart, regardless of their substance. The best we can offer Him is to give unselfishly the gift of our total selves. "I beseech you therefore, brethren, by the mercies of God, that ye present your bodies a living sacrifice, holy, acceptable unto God, which is your reasonable service" (Romans 12:1).

Give of your best to the Master;
Give Him first place in your heart;
Give Him first place in your service,
Consecrate ev'ry part.

Give, and to you shall be given;
God His beloved Son gave;
Gratefully seeking to serve Him,
Give Him the best that you have.
                                        – Howard B. Grose

Abel, the Voice From Beyond the Grave

And the Lord had respect unto Abel and to his offering (Genesis 4:4).

INTRODUCTION

Abel, son of Adam and Eve, became the first of the human family to die, fulfilling the death sentence passed upon mankind. His death however, was not a result of his own sin, but that of his jealous, murderous brother, Cain.

I. THE CHARACTER OF GODLY ABEL

A. A Keeper of the Sheep

   1. Scriptural shepherds: Abraham, Moses, David, Amos, Jesus Christ

   2. Qualities of a shepherd *(Genesis 12:16; Exodus 3:1; 1 Samuel 16:11; Amos 7:14; John 10:14)*

     a. A shepherd is unselfish *(John 10:1-10)*.

     b. A shepherd is sacrificial.

     c. A shepherd is loving.

B. Abel's More Excellent Sacrifice

   1. The offering was the best of his flock *(Genesis 4:4)*.

   2. The offering was a life given *(Hebrews 9:22)*.

Outline

   3. The offering was given willingly.

   4. The offering was given in faith (*Hebrews 11:4*).

C. Cain's Offering

   1. It could have been accepted.

   2. God accepted both "meat" and "meal" offerings (*Genesis 18:6; Ezekiel 45:24*).

   3. Apparently, his life was not consistent with his offering (*Genesis 4:5*).

   4. He would not receive divine instruction about his attitude (*Genesis 4:6-8*).

II. THE CONSEQUENCES OF UNBRIDLED ANGER

A. The Death of Cain's Brother, Abel

   1. Premeditated (*Genesis 4:8*)

   2. Covered up (*Genesis 4:10*)

B. The Curse on Him and His Descendants (*Genesis 4:11*)

   1. Immediate

   2. Lasting

III. THE VOICE OF ABEL'S TESTIMONY

A. A Six-fold Message from the Grave (*Hebrews 11:4*)

B. A Testimony of Faith Lives Forever (*Hebrews 11:6*)

C. Abel's True Gift—His Personal Devotion to God

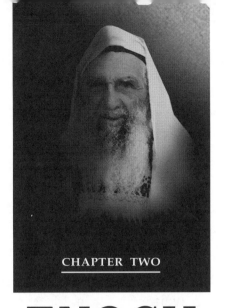

CHAPTER TWO

ENOCH
Walking to Please God

Enoch walked with God: and he was not; for God took him
(Genesis 5:24).

ENOCH IS A UNIQUE CHARACTER IN THE BIBLE. The few glimpses we are given of this special man reveal him to be an extraordinary human being. Brief is the view, but majestic is the picture of this outstanding saint!

In a day of shallow characters and forgotten integrity, Enoch is a sight for sore eyes. Living seven generations from Adam, Enoch descended from Adam through the line of Seth. He is the first man after Cain about whom the Bible reflects or makes a comment. That comment, found in Genesis 5:24, is of such power and significance that it reverberates throughout Scripture.

Enoch rose quickly from a company of obscure early humans to become a patriarch and prophet of renown. This man left such an impact that he is named by three different writers in the New Testament (Luke 3:37; Hebrews 11:5; Jude 14).

Some of the words of his eternal prophecy are quoted by the writer in Jude 14, 15; and there is strong prophetical speculation that he will be one of the two witnesses during the Great Tribulation period mentioned in Revelation 11:1-12.

In a true sense Genesis 5:24 is a short and concise, yet powerful, biography. It seems impossible for a single sentence to adequately describe 365 years, but in this case this verse does exactly that.

ENOCH EXPERIENCED GOD

How interesting it is to note that the Bible says Enoch walked with God. The actual Hebrew word *halak* means to have a conversant walk, or to walk before or in the presence of a walking companion.

The Bible first mentions Enoch's walk with God after the birth of his son, Methuselah (Genesis 5:22). Some scholars say that the very name of Methuselah is significant in that it is purported to mean, "when he is dead it shall come."

It is likely that the birth of Methuselah and the giving of his name was the result of a profound experience with God that Enoch received. The name he gave his son indicates he had received prophetic revelation and was deeply moved by the Lord.

Immediately after Methuselah's birth the Word declares, "And Enoch walked with God." The naming of Enoch's son therefore, was a prophetic act. Methuselah was the grandfather of Noah and died the year the flood came.

Every sovereign move of God in our lives should draw us into a walking relationship with Him! Enoch must have been given a glimpse of the impending deluge of judgement that would come in Noah's day.

Perhaps he saw around him the godless atmosphere that was developing so rapidly. The sin of Eden was deep in the fertile ground of the human heart, and Enoch knew no cure could be found outside of a relationship with Jehovah.

ENOCH WALKED WITH GOD

Seeing the times in which he lived, Enoch began his fateful and profitable journey to a wonderful destiny.

The Hebrew word for God in Genesis 5:24 is *Elohim* meaning "the Supreme God." Perhaps idolatry had become rampant, and it was necessary to point out that Enoch walked with the one and only true God.

His walk was a solitary walk, but not a lonely one. Others may casually stroll with false deities and walk hand-in-hand with idols, but not Enoch.

Others might embrace Baal and cling to the bosom of Ashtorath, but Enoch walked with the true God of heaven.

Oh, for such men and women in this hour!

Although they are extremely popular, the idol gods of luxury and affluence offer no solace for the child of God. True believers do not waste their steps and spend their days conversing with the gods and goddesses of the flesh, for they know that their God is a jealous God.

This was the conviction of Enoch. The trends of the time cannot move a man or woman who walks with God. Enoch had a prophetic encounter with God at age 65 (Genesis 5:21), and he was never the same again.

Enoch was not to be the last person to have such a life-changing encounter, however. One day, an 80-year-old shepherd looked up at the side of a mountain deep in the wilderness of Midian. One day he saw a bush that burned, yet was not consumed—and was never the same after that.

Shoeless, Moses stood in the presence of the same God Enoch walked with. He offered both his staff and his life to this matchless God (see Exodus 3:1-6).

A statesman-prophet and dignified orator of renown, Isaiah stood in the temple at Jerusalem in a time of profound national grief and saw the Lord high and lifted up.

The Lord was surrounded by sacred seraphim, and the smoke of God's glory filled the house.

While the posts of the doors trembled at the sound of God's voice, Isaiah cried that cry of submission that echoes down the centuries, "Here am I; send me" (Isaiah 6:8).

Enoch, Moses and Isaiah all encountered the presence of God and walked willingly thereafter in His continuous presence. Walking with God was their very lives. They lived to walk, and their talk never conflicted with their walk.

Now not only was Enoch's walk with God inspired and motivated by a prophetical encounter, but it was a walk "before" God. In other words, Enoch's life was such that he could walk before God with a total absence of shame.

ENOCH PLEASED GOD

The writer of the Book of Hebrews described Enoch's life beautifully when he declared, "For before his translation he had this testimony, that he pleased God" (Hebrews 11:5).

Others may live to please men or the rules of a certain culture that surrounds them, but not the true child of God.

Those who seek to be "men pleasers" must do as the men they seek to please require. When men and women live to climb into the higher echelons of their culture, regardless of what that culture is, then they do as the culture requires. Hence, the world is filled with dishonest and crooked politicians.

Our society is a sea of refuse and debauchery, and those who live to please the world are adrift in it. No wonder the apostle John was so poignant in his cry of warning against living to please this world. Hear his tirade in 1 John 2:15-17:

> Love not the world, neither the things that are in the world. If any man love the world, the love of the Father is not in him. For all that is in the world, the lust of the flesh, and the lust of the eyes, and the pride of life, is not of the Father, but is of the world. And the world

passeth away, and the lust thereof: but he that doeth the will of God abideth forever.

Enoch knew he could not please God and please the world at the same time, so he walked before God to please Him alone.

The writer of Hebrews gives us more insight into the depth of Enoch's character when he tells us in 11:6, "But without faith it is impossible to please [God]." Enoch had faith. He could never have pleased God otherwise. In fact, the Bible gives us some sound examples of Enoch's faith in God.

Enoch had a prophetic faith. Jude tells us that Enoch prophesied of the second return of Christ to the earth.

And Enoch also, the seventh from Adam, prophesied of these, saying, Behold, the Lord cometh with ten thousands of his saints, To execute judgement upon all, and to convince all that are ungodly among them of all their ungodly deeds which they have ungodly committed, and of all their hard speeches which ungodly sinners have spoken against him (Jude 14, 15).

Here a prophet of God who lived millennia before Christ's first coming prophesies of His second return.

Not only does he prophesy of Christ's second return, but he prophesies of divine justice that will take place at this return as God deals with sin and rebellion.

This prophecy was from a man who walked before God and pleased God by faith. He received this word of prophecy by faith and proclaimed it by faith.

We need such men and women in this stage of the church's sojourn on earth. Heroes of the faith are now at a premium. We need prophets who will prophesy under the anointed unction of the Holy Spirit, and who fear not the consequences of rejection by a carnal society or church.

Has the church culture of the last days become so "Laodicean" (see Revelation 3:14-18) in its attitude that it is declaring, "We have need of nothing?"

Do we despise "prophesyings" and laugh with disdain at "words from the Lord?"

Are we so concerned with denominational structure and positions of ecclesiastical power within the church that we no longer yearn for burning bushes and the cry of the seraphim?

Positions of human manufacture can never replace the offices of evangelist, pastor, prophet, apostle and teacher that God ordained for his church. These are offices of and by faith. The holders of these positions do what they do to please God and God alone. They are not of this world nor do they fit here comfortably.

Enoch prophesied as he was commanded and everything he did was to please the Lord.

ENOCH WAS TRANSLATED

Finally, Enoch was translated. He escaped the pain of death. God chose to translate him, which means that God raptured Enoch into His presence.

For thousands of years now, Enoch has been in the presence of God. Here we have a type and shadow of the kind of person who will be ready for the rapture of the church. The qualities can be listed, for all are found in the life of this man, Enoch.

The following characteristics can be found in the lives of "rapture-ready" people:

1. They are people of faith (Hebrews 11:6).

2. They live to please God (Hebrews 11:5).

3. They proclaim the truth (Jude 14).

4. They seek an encounter with God (Genesis 5:24).

5. They believe in the reality of God (Hebrews 11:6).

6. They diligently seek Him (Hebrews 11:6).

Enoch completed his walk with God. Yet, as he departed this world for the splendors of eternity, he left something behind: Enoch left his testimony.

Some leave great fortunes of wealth and others leave volumes of heady writ. Still others leave legendary stories of their feats of skill and heroic strength. Enoch, however, left more than any of these.

This righteous man of faith left an unblemished and powerful testimony. The writer of Hebrews says it best in pure and simple language, "He had this testimony, that he pleased God" (Hebrews 11:5).

May that be our testimony. May God forbid us to settle for less.

And He walks with me, and He talks with me,
And He tells me I am His own;
And the joy we share as we tarry there,
None other has ever known.

-C. Austin Miles

Outline

Enoch, Walking to Please God

Enoch walked with God: and he was not; for God took him (Genesis 5:24).

INTRODUCTION

Enoch is an extremely unique character in the Bible in that the few glimpses we are given of him reveal an extraordinary human being. "Brief is the view, but majestic is the picture," so to speak.

In a day of shallow characters and forgotten integrity, Enoch is a sight for sore eyes.

I. ENOCH EXPERIENCED GOD.

A. Enoch was the seventh man from Adam of the line of Seth *(Genesis 5:18)*.

1. He is the first man the sacred scriptures comment on *(Genesis 5:22)*.

2. His son's name indicates a prophetic encounter with God *(Genesis 5:21)*.

3. Jude refers to Enoch as a prophet *(Jude 14)*.

Outline

4. The Bible indicates Enoch began his walk with God with this prophetic encounter *(Genesis 5:22)*.

   a. Moses began at the burning bush *(Exodus 3:10)*.

   b. Isaiah began in the Temple *(Isaiah 6:8)*

II. ENOCH WALKED WITH GOD.

   A. Enoch walked with the true God.

   1. The word for God in Genesis 5:22 is *Elohim*.

   2. Men walk with those whom they wish to please *(Amos 3:3)*.

   3. Enoch wanted to please God *(Hebrews 11:5)*.

   B. Enoch's walk was one of faith *(Hebrews 11:6)*.

   1. His walk was diligent *(Hebrews 11:6)*.

   2. His walk was holy. One cannot walk with a Holy God without being holy.

III. ENOCH PLEASED GOD (Hebrews 11:5).

   A. To please the world and please God at the same time is an impossibility *(1 John 2:15-17)*.

   B. There is a danger in living to please a religious culture and not God. The Pharisees were guilty of this *(Matthew 23:1-33)*.

   C. Since God is the final judge and not earthly men, true children of God should live as Enoch, and live to please Him *(Ecclesiastes 12:13, 14)*.

Outline

IV. ENOCH WAS TRANSLATED (*Genesis 5:24; Hebrews 11:5*).

A. Enoch is a type of the "rapture-ready" saint.

1. People whose lives please God are in the truest sense of the words "rapture ready."

2. Enoch's translation was instantaneous. The Bible simply says, "He was not" (*Genesis 5:24*).

3. The rapture will also be instantaneous for all who are walking with God (*1 Thessalonians 4:17*).

CHAPTER THREE

ABRAHAM
The Friend of God

But thou, Israel, art my servant, Jacob whom I have chosen,
the seed of Abraham my friend (Isaiah 41:8).

IT IS SAID THAT FEW TRUE FRIENDS are acquired in a lifetime. Acquaintances may be many, but the term "friend" can be applied to only a select few.

For the almighty God who inhabits eternity to identify a mortal as His friend is a happening of great significance. Yet, in this inspiring text, God Almighty identifies the man, Abraham, as His friend. God does this unashamedly. Almost boastfully He proclaims his relationship with Abraham as a friendship.

ABRAHAM, GOD'S FRIEND

In his classic prayer, when the multitudes of Ammon and Moab were sorely pressing against him in battle, King Jehoshaphat reminded God that he was of the seed of Abraham "thy friend" (see 2 Chronicles 20:7). Victory came swiftly for Jehoshaphat that day.

The apostle James wrote about Abraham's test of faith when he was asked to offer Isaac up to God. James referred to this righteous man's great act of faith by saying, "And he was called the Friend of God" (James 2:23).

What greater or more noble thing can be said about any man than to be referred to as "the Friend of God?" Titles such as King, Emperor, Potentate, President, Premier, Chief or Secretary-General pale in comparison to the title "Friend of God."

One does not become a friend of God through mundane things such as riches or blood lines. This title is not achieved through elections, rulings of parliament, or ecclesiastical declarations.

It comes only through a relationship with God Himself, our partner in the friendship. He chooses His friends at His own divine discretion, and His divine wisdom is the guideline for the choice. Earthly titles are forgotten with the scattering of the sands of time, but the friends of God are remembered forever.

The grave sites of royalty are but infrequent tourist attractions; God's friends are in His presence eternally and "shine as the brightness of the firmament" (Daniel 12:3).

TO BE GOD'S FRIEND

Abraham's life is a portrait of what it takes to be a "friend of God." And the surprising thing is that his life was not without human error and fleshly stumbling.

Be a Follower

The mistakes of his life are glaring, but his faith in God is so undaunted and his love for the Lord so real that they lift him above his own human frailty and enable his example of victory in the midst of adversity to sing to us across time.

Abraham was born in Ur of the Chaldees in the Euphrates Valley. This place was near what would become, in later centuries, the land of Babylon. At the death of Terah, his father, Abraham was told to leave that place and journey toward a land called Canaan (see Genesis 12:1).

He left the land of Ur with his father and his family, and they dwelt in a place called Haran.Verse 4 says, "So Abram departed, as the Lord had spoken unto him."

Be Obedient

This is our first insight into a characteristic that would mark Abraham all of his life—pure and simple obedience. Always, Abraham obeyed God.

There was never a question. No discussion. Arguments and counter-reasoning were never used by this former Chaldean.

He simply did what God told him to do. The cry of the hour from God's people is a cry for obedience.

Disobedience has brought us strife, heartbreak, carnality, spiritual impotence and barren altars. Sins are committed when we disobey. Churches are torn with strife, because of disobedience.

Lives are unfulfilled as men and women settle for less than God's will due to a lack of obedience. Homes become battlegrounds, because God's Word is disobeyed. Children rise up against parents, because of disobedience.

Jesus said in John 14:15, "If ye love me, keep my commandments." Samuel cried to King Saul, "Behold, to obey is better than sacrifice" (1 Samuel 15:22).

Paul told the Corinthian church that if they would prove their love toward God, they had to be "obedient in all things" (2 Corinthians 2:8, 9). Isaiah said, "If ye be willing and obedient, ye shall eat the good of the land" (Isaiah 1:19).

Abraham lived a life of obedience. When God told him to leave his home and journey to an unknown land, Abraham began his journey. When God told him to offer his son Isaac up for a burnt offering, he never disputed this unbelievable command. He simply obeyed!

Be Faithful

How can one obey so unquestionably, unless that person knows the nature of the commander? Abraham knew God; they were friends! As a friend, Abraham had submitted himself to God's Lordship over his life.

Such men become giants of the faith. God said to *Joshua*, "Arise, go over this Jordan. . . . Every place that the soles of your foot shall tread upon, that have I given unto you" (Joshua 1:2, 3). No hesitation betrayed Joshua; he was obedient. He crossed the Jordan at God's command (see Joshua 3:17).

God told *Elijah* to go to a poor widow's house in the midst of a drought-ravaged, famine-plagued land. His promise to Elijah borders on the ridiculous to one who doesn't have an intimate knowledge of God, for God promised, "I have commanded a widow woman there to sustain thee." (1 Kings 17:9).

What sustenance can be found in poverty? What provision can one find among the starving? But Elijah never hesitatesd. "So he arose and went to

Zarephath" (v. 10). His knowledge of God left no room for anything but obedience.

Philip was told to leave a great citywide revival in Samaria and go to a deserted wilderness in Gaza (see Acts 8:26). Verse 27 says, "And he arose and went."

Human reasoning was cast aside, for what sense does it make to leave the crowds, the excitement and the exuberance of the masses who are listening to your message, and to journey into an unknown desert devoid of people and the means of livelihood?

No hesitation could be found in evangelist Philip! God had His reasons for the move, and that was enough for Philip.God's deserts are always better than our paradises. His barren ground is waiting for our seed-nurturing rain of total obedience.

Philip's single convert in the desert is a man of such distinction that as a newborn Christian, he shook the nation of Ethiopia for Christ. Obedience impresses God more than any achievement could ever begin to impress Him!

Be Devoted

We know that Abraham was God's friend because of the profound devotion he had for God. The Bible says, "A friend loveth at all times" (Proverbs 17:17). There was no period in Abraham's life when his devotion and love for God waned.

His devotion was best expressed in his worship of God. In Genesis 12:8, Abraham is seen building an altar to God on a mountain east of Bethel. Coming out of Egypt, he stops at this altar and calls on the name of the Lord (13:4).

Abraham and Lot were divided by a disagreement, and Abraham moved to the barren plains of Mamre in Hebron. His first act there was to build an altar to the Lord (see v. 18).

On Mt. Moriah's lofty heights he is found, in obedience to God, building an altar to offer up Isaac. Abraham was a praying man.

His cries to God reverberate throughout the Book of Genesis. In chapter 17, he joined himself and his household with God in the covenant of circumcision.

Abraham never staggered at the promise of God through unbelief, although he was nearly 100-years-old and his barren wife was about 90 when it was made. Instead, he readily accepted God's covenant to make of his seed a nation through which all the earth would be blessed (see Genesis 17:1-5).

Paul gives a powerful commentary on why Abraham was willing at God's command to offer up Isaac as a sacrifice (see Romans 4:19, 20). Hebrews 11:17-19 says, "By faith Abraham, when he was tried, offered up Isaac: and he that had received the promises offered up his only begotten son, Of whom it was said, That in Isaac shall thy seed be called: Accounting that God was able to raise him up, even from the dead."

What a testimony of unshakable devotion and faith in God! There are no doubts here. No wonder God calls this man "My friend."

Our hour desperately needs a revival of devotion to God. Jesus said, "For where your treasure is, there will your heart be also" (Luke 12:34).

Could it be that men's treasures have changed and as they have changed, there has been a changing of the heart? To walk in the light as He is in the light means He must be our light. To focus on Him means He is your treasure, the apple of your eye and the object of your affection.

Abraham was a sojourner of the bedouin tradition and he could travel no place without building an altar, for where he dwelt, he had to worship. There is no substitute for devotion in a "friend relationship" with God.

In fact, He will accept no less. Be assured that Abraham was devoted to God.

FRIENDS COMMUNICATE

True friends must communicate for the friendship to keep growing. God and Abraham talked together a lot. They didn't keep secrets from each other.

It was impossible for Abraham anyway, for God is omniscient; but we read an interesting passage in Genesis 18:17, where God asks, "Shall I hide from Abraham that thing which I do?" Imagine God contemplating a decision based on His friendship with a human!

God intended to destroy Sodom for its terrible wickedness. Abraham's nephew, Lot, along with Lot's family, were citizens of Sodom. God had every right to annihilate that evil city and tell no one of His plans. He is absolutely sovereign.

But because of His love and friendship for Abraham, He told him beforehand of Sodom's impending doom. This act gave Abraham a chance to plead for mercy on behalf of his nephew. Lot and his daughters were saved as a direct result of Abraham's friendship with God and the communication that resulted from that friendship.

Friendship with God is a relationship tied together with communications. Prayer was a signal trait in the lives of Biblical saints. God's friends talk to Him . . . and they see the results of their prayers.

✓ Hannah prayed for a son until she could only murmur (1 Samuel 11:12-13).

✓ Elijah's prayer on Mt. Carmel consisted of 63 words that brought immediate heavenly attention (1 Kings 18:36-38).

✓ Hezekiah' and Isaiah's prayer brought the overnight

angelic destruction of Sennacherib and Assyria (2 Chronicles 32:21).

✓ Samson's prayer, "Remember me," was all God needed to hear as He avenged Samson of the Philistines (Judges 16:28).

✓ Jesus' Gethsemane prayer enabled Him to bear the sins of the world to Golgotha. (Matthew 26:42).

THE FATHER OF THE FAITHFUL

Abraham's friendship was deeply rooted in faith and faithfulness. Because of his loyalty to God, he is often referred to as the "father of the faithful."

Did Abraham make mistakes? Most certainly. In Egypt he feared Pharaoh and tried to pass Sarah off as his sister instead of his wife in order to save his own life. Here he failed to trust God.

On another occasion both he and Sarah became impatient while waiting on the son of promise. At Sarah's request, Abraham had a relationship with Hagar as his surrogate wife. Ishmael was a result of this tryst, and the contention between the descendants of Ishmael and Isaac has plagued the world for centuries.

The point is, Abraham was not divine and he failed on occasion, but God never renounced their friendship. In fact, the covenant God made with

Abraham in Genesis 12:3 ("And I will bless them that bless thee, and curse him that curseth thee") is still in effect today.

History has proven many times that those who fight, curse and try to destroy the seed of Abraham are themselves judged of God. But those who bless Abraham's seed have seen God's blessings poured out upon them in great measure.

God doesn't forget His friends. When one considers the depth of the promise Jesus made to His disciples in John 15:14-15, he or she realizes the great treasures found in discipleship.

Listen to the Master's promise of the richness in having a friendship with God: "Ye are my friends, if ye do whatsoever I command you. Henceforth I call you not servants; for the servant knoweth not what his lord doeth: but I have called you friends; for all things that I have heard of my Father I have made known unto you."

What a Friend we have in Jesus,
All our sins and griefs to bear!
What a privilege it is to carry,
Ev'rything to God in prayer.

– Joseph Scriven

Abraham, the Friend of God

But thou, Israel, art my servant, Jacob whom I have chosen, the seed of Abraham my friend (Isaiah 41:8).

INTRODUCTION

It has been said that a person acquires few true friends in a lifetime. Acquaintances may be many, but the term *friend* can be applied to only a select few. For the God who inhabits eternity to identify a mortal man as His friend is a happening of great significance.

Yet, in this inspiring text, God Almighty identifies Abraham as His friend. God does this unashamedly. Almost boastfully He proclaims His relationship with Abraham as that of friend.

I. ABRAHAM WAS THE FRIEND OF GOD.

  A. Scripture testifies to this friendship.

    1. *Isaiah 41:8*: "The seed of Abraham my friend"

    2. *2 Chronicles 20:7*: "Abraham, thy friend"

    3. *James 2:23*: "And [Abraham] was called the Friend of God."

  B. "The friend of God" is the best of titles.

    1. All earthly titles pale in comparison to this one; they are all temporary (*2 Corinthians 4:18*).

    2. God chooses His friends (*John 15:16*).

Outline

II. WHAT IT TAKES TO BE A FRIEND OF GOD

A. Be a follower.

1. God knows us (*Psalms 103:14*).

2. God forgives us (*Psalms 25:18*).

B. Be obedient.

1. He left Ur at God's command (*Genesis 12:4*).

2. Obedience is a sign of love (*John 14:15*).

3. Obedience is preferred above sacrifice (*1 Samuel 15:22*).

4. Obedience brings reward (*Isaiah 1:19*).

C. Be faithful.

1. Joshua crossed a flooded river at God's command (*Joshua 3:17*).

2. Elijah the prophet sought sustenance from an impoverished widow at God's command (*1 Kings 17:9, 10*).

3. Philip left a successful revival and went to the desert at God's command (*Acts 8:26, 27*).

D. Be devoted.

1. "A friend loveth at all times" (*Proverbs 17:17*).

2. Abraham was an altar builder (*Genesis 12:8; 13:4, 18; 22:9*).

3. A revival of devotion is the crying need of this hour (*2 Chronicles 7:14*).

Outline

III. ABRAHAM COMMUNICATED WITH GOD.

 A. True friends communicate (*Amos 3:3*).

 B. God told Abraham of Sodom's impending destruction (*Genesis 18:17*).

 C. Friendship is a communicative relationship (*Judges 16:28; 1 Kings 18:36-38; Matthew 26:42*).

IV. ABRAHAM BECAME THE FATHER OF THE FAITHFUL.

 A. His faith was only in God (*Hebrews 11:17-19*).

 B. Abraham had God's trust (*Genesis 18:19*).

 C. Abraham led his entire household into a covenant relationship with God (*Genesis 17:23*).

 D. God pronounced an eternal blessing on Abraham and his seed (*Genesis 12:3*).

V. CONCLUSION: THROUGH CHRIST WE BECOME THE FRIENDS OF GOD

 A. Jesus made this wonderful promise of friendship (*John 15:14-15*).

 B. We are Abraham's seed by faith (*Galatians 3:7*).

CHAPTER FOUR

JACOB

The Limping Prince

And he said, Thy name shall be called no more Jacob, but Israel: for as a prince hast thou power with God and with men, and hast prevailed (Genesis 32:28).

FEW CHARACTERS IN THE BIBLE PORTRAY HUMANITY, at its worst and at its best, as vividly as Jacob. This grandson of Abraham is the consummate human, complete with failures and triumphs. Yet, in spite of human weaknesses, Jacob prevails with God and becomes a channel of blessing to the people of earth as he fathers the 12 tribes of Israel.

These tribes included Judah, from whom Jesus Christ, the Savior of the world, would descend. Throughout Scripture, God continually identified Himself as "the God of Jacob." This grandson of Abraham has a story worth listening to.

JACOB'S HISTORY

Jacob was one of the twin sons born to Isaac and Rebekah. During Rebekah's pregnancy, God spoke to her and told her that the twin sons she would bear represented two nations in her womb (see Genesis 25:23).

God also told her in the same verse that the elder son would be subservient to the younger. At their birth the first son was born and named Esau. It is significant that the second infant, Jacob, took hold of Esau's heel as he came out of his mother's birth canal (v. 26).

The Bible describes the development of the two boys in verse 27. Esau was a hunter and a man of the fields; while Jacob was a plain man, dwelling in tents, a keeper of sheep and goats.

We soon learn of Jacob's cunning, however, when he took advantage of his brother's hunger and lack of character depth. The famished and hungry Esau sold Jacob his precious birthright and was never able to regain it (see Hebrews 12:16, 17).

The name "Jacob," pronounced *Yahakobe* in the Hebrew, literally means "a supplanter." According to Webster's dictionary, *supplant* means "to displace and take the place of." Jacob fulfilled the prophecy of his name, for he received, through his deception, the birthright blessing that was to be bestowed by the father to the eldest son.

His mother, Rebekah, was a willing partner in this deception. Although Esau was the victim, his own carnal foolishness brought about the disfavor of the Lord and his loss of stature (see Romans 9:13).

While Jacob's deception of his father Isaac is flagrant (see Genesis 27:15-23), it is in his acquiring of the birthright that we find an admirable quality in Jacob. *He had a desire for the things that really mattered.*

His subtle and deceptive method of obtaining his father's blessing was reprehensible, but the fact that he wanted it is admirable.

This powerful desire in Jacob for the blessing of birthright helps us to understand why God in His sovereignty chooses whom and what He chooses. Paul deals with this subject extensively in Romans 9.

He reminds us that God loved Jacob and hated Esau (v. 13). He also tells us that God in His sovereignty has compassion and mercy on whom He chooses (v. 15). Paul uses the illustration of the potter and the potter's power over the lump of clay to make vessels of honor or dishonor (v. 21).

Jacob's Admirable Qualities

God, who knows our lives and the character qualities in them, chooses us for the tasks and roles that best bring Him glory and benefits His creation. God chose Jacob and rejected Esau, but each individual made choices that molded their lives.

Jacob Chose Wisely

After the death of Isaac, Esau swore vengeance on Jacob, and Jacob had to flee his homeland or forfeit his life (see Genesis 27:41-45). In his flight from Esau's wrath, we see the molding hand of the divine Potter in the life of Jacob.

Weary for sleep he stops in his flight to rest, arranging rocks for a pillow. In a dream that night, he envisioned a ladder reaching from earth to heaven with the angels of God ascending and descending upon it.

At the ladder's heavenly crest stood the Lord, who told him that the land he slept on would be given to him and his seed, that his descendants would be spread as "the dust of the earth," and that "in thy seed shall all the families of the earth be blessed" (28:14).

God also promised him that He would be with him wherever he went. He said that He would never leave him until He had done all He had promised (v. 15).

Jacob's stone pillows became an oil-anointed monument, and he named the place Bethel, meaning "the house of God."

Jacob Asked Largely

Jacob asked God to be his provision and let him return in peace. He vowed to give God a tenth of all He received. But it is interesting to note that Jacob did not leave without asking for the blessings of God in return for His devotion.

To some this might seem arrogant or demanding, but we should view this as an example of Jacob's faith. He had heard the stories of God's faithfulness to his grandfather, Abraham, and to his father, Isaac. In a dream He had just heard God's personal promise to bless him and his seed.

Believing the glorious promise, Jacob acted on his faith and asked for provisions, safety and a return to his homeland in peace. God appreciates the boldness of petitioners. The Bible is replete with examples of those who asked God for things and received them.

Here are some scriptures from the Word on the

necessity and the importance of asking big . . . of asking with an adventurous faith:

✓ James said, "Ye have not, because ye ask not" (James 4:2).

✓ Jesus said, "'If ye shall ask anything in my name, I will do it'" (John 14:14).

✓ The apostle John said, "And whatsoever we ask, we receive of him, because we keep his commandments, and do those things that are pleasing in his sight" (1 John 3:22).

✓ Solomon asked for wisdom and God granted it (1 Kings 3:11, 12).

✓ Elijah asked for rain and it came in abundance (1 Kings 18:45).

✓ Bartimeus asked for sight and suddenly he saw (Mark 10:51, 52).

Jesus told of a powerful, unjust judge who granted a poor widow woman a request simply because she kept asking. This judge feared neither God nor man, but the widow kept asking until she wearied the judge into granting her request (Luke 18:2-8).

God invites us to "Come boldly unto the throne of grace, that we may obtain mercy, and find grace to help in time of need" (Hebrews 4:16).

Such was Jacob's boldness with God. He would not leave such a holy place without petitioning the

God of all provision. Jacob was a seeker. He looked for an opportunity to embrace the birthright blessing from Isaac, and now he sought the Lord at Bethel for His blessing and protection on his life.

Jacob Remembered Conspicuously

Jacob was also a man who believed in making memorials. He forever memorialized the place of the dream by calling it Bethel, which literally means, "The house of God." He returned 30 years later to renew his covenant at that place, renaming it El-Bethel, which means "God in the House of God."

He memorialized the stones he slept on, erecting them as a pillar of memory and anointing them with oil. The stones themselves would symbolize the permanence, while the oil represents the anointed presence of God.

✓ Moses built a famous memorial at Mt. Sinai (Exodus 24:4).

✓ Joshua built a memorial of stones at the Jordan River (Joshua 4) and at Shechem (24:26).

✓ Samuel set up a memorial to remember the victory of the Philistines in 1 Samuel 7:12.

God allows memorials, but never idols; and there is a vast difference. Biblical memorials commemorate God's acts and blessings; idols were and are built to honor false gods.

The memory of God's might and power builds faith. Jacob further memorialized this event at Bethel by making a vow, albeit conditional, to make the Lord his God forever and to pay tithe to the Lord. Bethel had impacted Jacob's life and he would never be the same.

Jacob Persisted Determinedly

A final aspect of Jacob's life was his undaunted determination. Against all odds, his trickery had gotten him the birthright, but it was sheer determination that would carry him through much of his life. The Texas Rangers have a saying, "It's hard to stop a determined man who believes right is on his side."

Jacob left Bethel and came to Haran. Beside a great well where thirsty sheep watered, he met Rachel, the great love of his life. Jacob agreed with her father, Laban, to work seven years for her hand in marriage (see Genesis 29:18).

One of the most beautiful commentaries on the love between a man and a woman is found in this story. The Bible says, "And Jacob served seven years for Rachel; and they seemed unto him but a few days, for the love he had to her" (v. 20).

Here we see Jacob's determination in his quest for Rachel and the depth of love in his heart for her.

Her father's trickery caused him to have to serve seven additional years for her hand, for custom dictated that the older daughter must marry before the younger.

Therefore, Jacob had to marry Rachel's older sister, Leah, first (v. 26). With Rachel and Leah, Jacob would father 12 sons and a daughter named Dinah.

Although his father-in-law, Laban, tried greedily to impoverish him, his covenant with God at Bethel brought great prosperity into his life. God literally overcame the laws of nature to increase the flocks and herds of Jacob (see vv. 37-43).

Laban's anger and jealousy toward him encouraged Jacob to go back to the land of Canaan, where Abraham's descendants were destined to dwell.

During Jacobs's sojourn back to Canaan, he faced the fact that he would have to see Esau again. His hostile twin was coming to meet him with 400 armed men. When he had left Esau years earlier, his brother's death threat was between them (see 27:41).

But as he approached Canaan, he met a host of angels. He called the place *Mahanaim*, meaning "two camps," for the angelic camp was on both sides of Jacob, assuring him that wherever he went he was under the divine protection promised at Bethel (see 32:2).

Human fear gripped Jacob like a vise. No

amount of miraculous intervention seemed to stifle his fears. Again we see Jacob's human side. He sent his entire family and all of his wealth before him to face Esau first. Perhaps he thought that their presence would soften Esau's heart.

Then the Bible says, "And Jacob was left alone" (v. 24).

Alone. The word itself is filled with a solitary sound, but in this solitary state many people find strength in God.

✓ Moses was alone on Mt. Sinai when He saw the back parts of God (Exodus 33:23).

✓ Isaiah was alone in the temple the year King Uzziah died, when he saw the Lord high and lifted up (Isaiah 6:1).

✓ Jesus was alone in the wilderness when He won His great victory over the devil (Matthew 4:1-11).

✓ John was alone as an exile on Patmos' rocky isle when he received the Revelation (Revelation 1:9).

Sometimes it is important to be separated from all distractions in order for God to deal with us as He needs to. Our attention cannot be divided if God is going to have preeminence in our lives.

Jacob's family was gone. The night was dark and the faint sounds made by the babbling of the brook, Jabbok, was the only thing that broke the stillness of the night. Then the grappling began. The Bible says, "And there wrestled a man with him" (Genesis 32:24).

The word for "wrestle" here is the Hebrew word *abaq*, meaning a literal physical struggle, not just a struggle of the mind and emotions. Jacob's tenacity and dogged determination came alive at this time. The wrestling continued through the night, and grew in such intensity that the angel touched the hollow of Jacob's thigh and his hip was thrown out of joint (see v. 25).

This did nothing to stop Jacob's determination to hold on. All of his strength seemed to be in his upper body.

The angel cried, "Let me go, for the day breaketh!" (v. 26).

Jacob's answer is classic and has served as an example for men and women who want something from God. "I will not let thee go, except thou bless me" (v. 26).

Esau was on the other side of the brook with his army of trained thugs, and Jacob thought that life as he knew it would soon be altered forever. Jacob desperately needed God to help him. His mind was set in concrete, he stood on a solid foundation, his only hope was in God, and he would not let go until God blessed him.

Jacob Became a Prince of God

So the blessing came! Two names were changed that night: the name of the person and the name of the place. God gave to Jacob the name *Israel*, which literally means "prevailed as a prince."

He had been Jacob the usurper, Jacob the trickster, Jacob the master of subtlety; but now heaven views him as a prince.

What a portrait of ourselves. We were once lost in our trespasses and sins; our lives were portraits of deceit and transgression. But Paul, whose name was also changed when he became a Christian, said it best, "Now in Christ Jesus ye who sometimes were far off are made nigh by the blood of Christ" (Ephesians 2:13).

Peter said, "Which in time past were not a people, but are now the people of God: which had not obtained mercy, but now have obtained mercy" (1 Peter 2:10).

All of us can identify with Jacob because all of us reach those places where we need a night of wrestling until deliverance comes.

Another name change occurred in this scene. Jacob named the place of this powerful encounter, *Peniel*, which means "the face of God." Jacob said, "For I have seen God face to face, and my life is preserved." (Genesis 32:30). Preservation comes with the presence of God. Jacob now knew His life would be spared.

It was there as the sun was rising that God gave Jacob a permanent memorial to that night of miracles. The Bible says that Jacob "halted" or limped. The scripture says the "sinew shrank upon the hollow of the thigh.

With every step of his life, Jacob would remember what God had done for him. He was a prince who limped. His limping reminded him of his total dependence on God and also of the power of perseverance in prayer. Perhaps the scars of our sins should be looked upon as memorials to God's deliverance.

Jacob would never run again. He would limp to his brother Esau, expecting death; but he would go without fear.

The hand of the Lord was mighty upon this limping prince, however. When his big brother Esau saw Jacob, after years of festering hatred, the heart of the hairy and muscular Esau melted.

"And Esau ran to meet him, and embraced him, and fell on his neck, and kissed him: and they wept" (33:4).

At Peniel a name was changed, and a lifelong grudge was shattered. The power of love prevailed for the two brothers.

What we often fear most, when turned in the hands of God, becomes the sweetest of blessings. The God of Heaven desires to turn our enemies and those with whom we have misunderstandings into embraceable brothers and sisters.

Often, the only thing preventing this miracle is our own stubbornness, and our lack of will. We have to be willing to seek the Lord and accept our lot with Him, even if it means acquiring a limp. Then we can embrace the one who is a foe no longer, but who now wears the badge of friend. The words of an old hymn says it best:

As Jacob in the days of old,
I wrestled with the Lord,
And instant with a courage bold,
I stood upon His word.

I would not be denied,
I would not be denied,
Till Jesus came and made me whole,
I would not be denied.

– C.P. Jones

Outline

Jacob, the Limping Prince

And he said, Thy name shall be called no more Jacob, but Israel: for as a prince hast thou power with God and with men, and has prevailed (Genesis 32:28).

INTRODUCTION

Few characters in the Bible portray humanity at its worst and at its best as vividly as Jacob does. He is the consummate human being, complete with failures and triumphs. Yet, despite human weaknesses, Jacob prevails with God and becomes the channel of blessing to the peoples of earth.

He fathered the 12 tribes of Israel, including Judah, from whom would descend Jesus Christ, the Savior of the world. Throughout the scriptures, God identifies Himself as "the God of Jacob." This grandson of Abraham has a story worth listening to.

I. JACOB'S HISTORY

A. The grandson of Abraham, a heritage of faith

B. A child of prophecy (*Genesis 25:23*)

C. His name meant "supplanter."

Outline

II. JACOB'S ADMIRABLE QUALITIES

A. Jacob chose wisely — he desired the things that really mattered.

1. He wanted the birthright (*Genesis 25:31*).

2. He wanted the blessing of his father (*Genesis 27:19*).

3. He wanted the favor of the Lord (*Genesis 28:20*).

4. He wanted divine protection (*Genesis 28:21*).

B. Jacob asked largely — he asked for God's special blessing in his vow at Bethel (*Genesis 28:20-22*). Here are some Biblical examples of asking largely:

1. Solomon (*1 Kings 3:5-11*)

2. Elijah (*1 Kings 18:36-38*)

3. Bartemaeus (*Mark 10:51-52*)

4. A poor widow (*Luke 18:2-8*)

C. Jacob remembered conspicuously — he believed in memorials.

1. He erected a pillar of remembrance at Bethel (*Genesis 28:22*).

2. Memorials were used throughout scripture:

   a. Moses at Sinai (*Exodus 20:4*)

   b. Joshua at Jordan (*Joshua 4*) and Shechem (*Joshua 24:26*)

   c. Samuel (*1 Samuel 7:12*)

Outline

D. Jacob persisted determinely—he never gave up his dreams or God's promises.

   1. He worked 14 years for Rachel (*Genesis 29:18*).

   2. He was persistent in building his herds (*Genesis 30:37-43*).

   3. He wrestled with an angel until he got an answer from God (*Genesis 32:24*).

III. JACOB BECAME A PRINCE WITH GOD.

A. His name was changed to *Israel*, which means "prevailing prince" (*Genesis 32:28*).

B. The place of his victory became known as *Peniel*, which means, "the face of God" (*Genesis 32:30*).

C. Jacob was given reconciliation with Esau.

   1. Love triumphed (*Genesis 33:4*).

   2. Jacob was given a permanent limp.

      a. His scar was one of victory.

      b. As an elder He would lean on his staff and bless Israel by faith (see *Hebrews 11:21*).

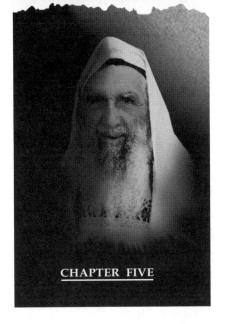

CHAPTER FIVE

CALEB
The Right Stuff

My servant Caleb, because he had another spirit with him, and hath followed me fully, him will I bring into the land whereinto he went; and his seed shall possess it (Numbers 14:24).

BECAUSE LITTLE IS WRITTEN ABOUT HIM, Caleb is one of the lesser-known characters in the Bible. This lack of attention does nothing to lessen his stature, however, for here is a man literally brimming with outstanding, godly character.

Caleb possessed boldness, intuition, powerful faith and rock-solid courage. He had keen intelligence and exhibited great leadership ability.

He so impressed the God of Israel that Jehovah labeled him "My servant Caleb." Of the Mosaic generation that left Egypt, only he and Joshua are allowed to enter the promised land. This privilege was given to them by God Himself as a result of their unshakable faith in Him.

CALEB'S BACKGROUND

Caleb was one of the original 12 spies who were chosen to go into the Promised Land to spy out the land (Numbers 13:6). He was a member of the tribe of Judah, and a comment on this fact is necessary in analyzing his life.

Judah is the tribe from which Israel's leadership would emerge. Boaz the husband of Ruth, David the son of Jesse, and Jesus the son of Mary would all be descendants of the tribe of Judah.

Jacob had prophesied, as he leaned on his staff, "The scepter shall not depart from Judah, nor a lawgiver from between his feet, until Shiloh come; and unto him shall the gathering of the people be" (Genesis 49:10).

Jacob also referred to Judah as a "lion" (v. 9). This meant that Judah and his descendants were people of power and cunning. These characteristics would be seen in men like Boaz and David. God chose this bloodline to produce the fleshly body of His son on this earth, and Jesus was a Man who inspired other men. From this tribe and lineage Caleb was born, and our first glimpses of him portray a leader of courage and fearlessness.

Caleb's father was an Israelite named Jephunneh. The name *Jephunneh* means "prepared." Surprisingly, the name *Caleb* means "bold." If indeed Caleb embodied the characteristics of the names of himself and his father, he was well suited to do exploits for God. Either trait without the other is sorely inadequate. But when one is well prepared and has the boldness to execute his preparedness, success is the likely result.

THE REPORT OF THE 10 SPIES

The 12 spies left the wilderness of Paran and journeyed into Canaan to spy out the land. When you look at the geographical span of their search, given in Numbers 13:21-23, you find that it was thorough and covered the entire territory.

At a brook called Eschol, in a rich valley south of Hebron, they cut down a huge cluster of grapes and two men were required to bear it. The search of Canaan and the reconaissance of their military objective lasted 40 days (v. 25).

When they arrived back in the camp of Israel, there was much excitement. All of the 12 spies agreed that the land was fruitful. "Surely it floweth with milk and honey" was their description (v. 27).

But this was the only thing the 12 agreed on. All of the spies except Joshua and Caleb began to tell about "walled cities," "the children of Anak," and the various "ites" — the Amelekites, Hittites, Jebusites and Amorites.

They said, "We be not able to go up against the people; for they are stronger than we" (Numbers 13:31). They told of men of great stature, giants and the "sons of Anak."

Sadly, they also reported their own poor self-esteem and lack of faith. They concluded their faithless report in verse 33 by saying, "And we were in our own sight as grasshoppers, and so we were in their sight."

What a dismal view! Had they forgotten the God of Abraham who had sent plagues on the most powerful nation of earth and delivered them from Pharaoh?

Had their memories of God's deliverance on the banks of the Red Sea dimmed? Was the taste of quail and manna so far removed from their lips that they couldn't remember God's provision? Had these people forgotten the power of the God of their fathers?

It would be easy for us to condemn them if our world of Christendom did not repeat their doubts so often. God gives us miracles of salvation, healing and deliverance; yet we forget the glorious past and doubt Him in the present.

We slide into ditches of depression and pull a cloak of despair around our shoulders as we view the circumstances around us, forgetting the One who is able to deliver us from those circumstances.

Can we recount a single time when God has failed? Does history record in its annals any instance, place or circumstance when God was the loser in a battle? Is the Bible true or just another classic work of literary genius?

CALEB'S AND JOSHUA'S REPORT

Where is our faith? We so often cast it aside and embrace the mantle of humanity. What we can see is easier to fear than what we can believe and yet not see!

In our vast struggles, we need to study men like Joshua and Caleb. In the midst of this report, Caleb spoke plainly, "And Caleb stilled the people before Moses, and said, Let us go up at once, and possess it; for we are well able to overcome it" (Numbers 13:30).

The "crowd" path is the easy path. Jesus said, "Wide is the gate, and broad is the way, that leadeth to destruction, and many there be which go in thereat" (Matthew 7:13).

Caleb could have joined the majority report and fit in well, but his faith would not be compromised by comfort. Caleb knew God; he had not forgotten God's ability.

This crowd wept that night in deep despair, convinced that all hope was gone (Numbers 14:1). They were ready to organize themselves and go back to Egypt (vv. 2-4).

Imagine people so faithless that they prefer a return to bondage and slavery over the conquest of the Promised Land!

Yet, in the truest sense of the word many are no different today. Rather than courageously walking by faith and totally depending on God, they enslave themselves to fleshly passions, carnal lifestyles, binding vices and habits, and the various gods of this world.

They find their comfort with the sinful masses and refuse to follow sandeled footprints of Jesus. Oh, for a return to a faith-walk lifestyle!

Another thing that distinguished Joshua and Caleb in their view of Canaan was the "absolute" factor in their faith. Doubt was totally foreign to these stalwart men of God. Listen to their report. It drips with the sweetness of unfeigned faith.

> If the Lord delight in us, then He will bring us into this land, and give it us; a land which floweth with milk and honey. Only rebel not ye against the Lord, neither fear ye the people of the land; for they are bread for us: their defense is departed from them, and the Lord is with us: fear them not (vv. 8-9).

These words are the blueprint for absolute victory. Victory is predicated on God's "delight" or pleasure in His people. "If," Caleb says, "the Lord delight in us," then He will give us this land and the victory to take it.

This condition is true in every conquest God's children face. We must live to please and delight God. Then there is nothing He will not do to bless His children.

The armies of earth, with all their power and prowess, are no match for the God of heaven. Riches to supply needs are within easy reach of the God of whom David said, "The earth is the Lords and the fulness thereof" (Psalm 24:1).

Caleb's heart and mind were filled with faith facts, and doubt is not to be found in him.

He then gives the warnings of a prophet for he says, "Only rebel not ye against the Lord, neither fear ye the people of the land" (v. 9). These two promises seem to go together. Rebellion against

God means regarding men more than God. The man, who obeys God fully, never fears the powers of men.

Caleb and Joshua rightly analyze the enemy. Listen to their startling and true report: "... for they are bread for us: their defense is departed from them, and the Lord is with us: fear them not" (Numbers 14:9).

Caleb and Joshua are saying literally, "We will swallow them as bread, they have no defense against the God we serve." What a statement of faith and resolve! How true it portrays all the enemies of God's people. All of His enemies are defenseless against the God of heaven.

Satan himself and the congregate masses and legions of hell's demonic forces have no power to stand before God. No wonder the apostle James declared, "Thou believest that there is one God; thou doest well: the devils also believe, and tremble" (James 2:19). Again he said, "Submit yourselves therefore to God. Resist the devil, and he will flee from you" (4:7).

One of the more regrettable moments in the history of Israel was when the people did not hearken to the advice and counsel of Joshua and Caleb. What a shame! The wrath of the Lord consumed that doubting generation in the wilderness. Only these two men of faith saw the Promise Land.

The Book of Hebrews tells us that the generation that doubted the report of Joshua and Caleb had within them "an evil of heart of unbelief" that made them depart from the living God (see 3:12). In fact, much of the third and fourth chapters of Hebrews deal with the consequences of the sin of unbelief.

God himself makes a beautiful comment about Caleb in Numbers 14:24. God calls him "my servant" in this verse — a title of love and of stature. Caleb, God says, "had another spirit with him," which had to be a spirit of devotion and faith.

Then God said, "He hath followed me fully," denoting the completeness of Caleb's devotion to God. No half-hearted gestures appear in the story of this man's life. Sold out completely to God, every fiber of his being was God-conscious, and he did not turn from the Lord or from God's purposes.

After 40 years of wilderness wandering and the death of the entire generation that doubted God, the time came for Israel to possess the land. At this moment, we are given another glimpse of Caleb.

CALEB RECEIVED HIS PROMISE

He is 85 years old now, but time has not weakened his resolve. Miraculously, neither his body nor his temperament has weakened. Hear the testimony of this senior citizen of renown as he steps up to claim his inheritance from God:

> And now behold, the Lord hath kept me alive, as he said, these forty and five years . . . and now, lo, I am this day fourscore and five years old. As yet I am as strong this day as I was in the day that Moses sent me: as my strength was then, even so is my strength now, for war, both to go out, and to come in.
>
> Now therefore give me this mountain, whereof the Lord spake in that day; for thou heardest in that day how the Anakims were there, and that the cities were great and fenced: if so be that the Lord will be with me, then I shall be able to drive them out, as the Lord said (Joshua 14:10-12).

This is a testimony to thrill the ages. Here is a man of God who is confident that his mission will be fulfilled. Caleb inherited Hebron and took it from the giants. The faithfulness of Caleb was rewarded with the faithfulness of God to him. God always rewards faith with faithfulness. Chapter 15 tells of Caleb's victories:

✓ In verses 14 and 15, he drove out the sons of Anak and conquered the city of Kirjathsepher, seven miles south of Hebron.

✓ The first judge of Israel, Othniel, became Caleb's son-in-law after he joined Caleb in battle against his enemies.

✓ Then Caleb's daughter demonstrated her father's attributes when she asked for a field and springs of water and promptly took it (vv.18, 19).

A father's faith passed on to his children is part of the great legacy of Caleb. A man who decided in his youth to "fully" follow the Lord found that in so doing he not only received an inheritance, but also secured the blessings of God for his descendants.

How often it is true that we give to our children what we ourselves acquire. We can only pass down what we have. Caleb had the "right stuff."

He gave the best back to those he loved. May God grant that we do likewise.

If you're in the battle for the Lord and right,
Keep on the firing line.
If you win my brother surely you must fight,
Keep on the firing line.
There are many dangers that we all must face,
If we die a fighting it is no disgrace,
Coward in the service, He will find no place,
So keep on the firing line.
—Otis L. McCoy

Caleb, the Right Stuff

*My servant Caleb, because he had another spirit with him,
and hath followed me fully, him will I bring into the land
whereinto he went; and his seed shall possess it*
(Numbers 14:24).

INTRODUCTION

Caleb is one of the lesser known, but more powerful characters in the Bible. Caleb had boldness, intuition, powerful faith, rock-solid courage, keen intelligence and great leadership ability. God was so impressed, He immediately identified him as "my servant Caleb."

I. CALEB'S BACKGROUND

A. He was one of the twelve spies of Israel to go into Canaan (*Numbers 13:6*).

B. He was of the tribe of Judah—the tribe from which Jesus would descend. Judah was a "lion's whelp."

C. Caleb's father's name, *Jephunneh,* means "prepared."

D. Caleb's name meant "bold." He possessed both boldness and preparedness.

Outline

II. THE REPORT OF THE TEN SPIES

A. The other spies believed Canaan unconquerable (*Number 13:31*).

B. The other spies had no faith and low self-esteem (*Numbers 13:33*).

C. This is the attitude of a weak, compromising, underachieving church (*Matthew 7:13*). The majority often feels this way.

III. CALEB AND JOSHUA'S REPORT

A. They agreed that the land flowed with milk and honey (*Numbers 13:27*).

B. They both believed it could be possessed at once (*Numbers 13:30*).

C. Their report was based upon their faith in God (*Numbers 14:8*).

D. Their faith saved them (*Numbers 14:30*).

IV. CALEB RECEIVED HIS PROMISE

A. Though 85 years of age, he was ready when his time came (*Joshua 14:10-12*).

B. Caleb took the land (*Joshua 15:14, 15*).

C. Caleb left an inheritance to his family (*Joshua 15:18-19*).

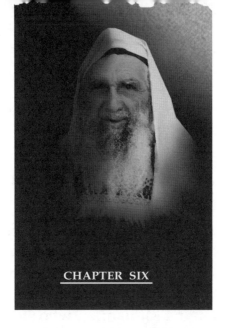

CHAPTER SIX

GIDEON
The Sword of the Lord

And what shall I more say? for the time would fail me to tell of Gideon (Hebrews 11:32)

WHEN GIDEON FIRST APPEARS ON THE BIBLICAL SCENE, he seems to be the most unlikely of heroic characters.

In fact he first comes to us as a poor, frustrated farm boy suffering from a total lack of self-esteem. His homeland is in ruins and under siege by a powerful militarized nation. He is discouraged and despondent because of the sad state of affairs around him.

Poverty and hunger rule the land and Gideon's people—God's people, the children of Israel—are hiding like frightened animals in caves and dens in the rocks.

Israel's Dilemma

Gideon was threshing wheat by a winepress to hide from the Midianites, Israel's enemies (Judges 6:11). We see the depth of despair that overshadowed the land, for the regular threshing floors of Israel could not be used because of the constant bands of foraging Midianites, who stole everything Israel produced.

The winepress at Ophrah was safe, for Israel had no grapes left. Besides, the Midianites would never suspect wheat was being threshed there. What a portrait of forlorn hopelessness!

Once-mighty Israel, descendants of Abraham, with the military traditions of Joshua and Caleb in their history, are now quaking in their sandals and hiding their meager sustenance from idol-worshiping foreigners.

Now this state of nationalistic trauma was not without reason. Like individuals, nations get into trouble when sin lies at the door. Judges 6:1 tells precisely the reason Israel was in this state. The scripture says, "And the children of Israel did evil in the sight of the Lord: and the Lord delivered them into the hand of Midian seven years."

Further, God had sent a prophet who reminded them that God was the One who delivered them out of Egypt and gave them the land of Canaan. He told them to never fear the idol gods of their enemies.

Through this prophet God told Israel what their sin was: "But ye have not obeyed my voice" (v. 10).

Disobedience, the diabolical sin behind all sins, had done in Israel. The wrath of the Lord had fallen like a flood of waters, and the people felt the chastisement of a God who loved them enough to turn their hearts back towards Him.

Their cry of despair in verse 7 brought the message of the prophet to them. In verse 11, God begins a miraculous deliverance through His encounter with the poor farm boy named Gideon.

Gideon's Qualities

He Was Humble.

The first thing you notice in the life of Gideon is his total humility before God. An angel appeared to him as he threshed wheat by the winepress at Ophrah, and told him, "The Lord is with thee, thou mighty man of valor!" (v. 12).

Gideon looked at his own rags, at the leanness of his ribs and his hidden wheat and asks the angel a reasonable question, "If the Lord be with us, why then is all this befallen us?" (v. 13).

He Was Prayerful.

He also asked where were all the miracles that his ancestors talked about, and why would God bring them from Egypt to deliver them to an equally cruel enemy like Midian?

The innocent are often victimized by the sins of those around them, and so it was with Gideon. His heart was pure and his questions sincere. Others had brought the judgement of God on the land; yet he, and innocents like him, were suffering with the disobedient.

God answered Gideon through the angel by telling him to go and save Israel. For, God said, "Have I not sent thee?" (v. 14). Gideon's humility, coupled with his low self-esteem, suddenly comes forth.

Gideon asks the angel, "Wherewith shall I save Israel? Behold my family is poor in Manasseh, and I am the least in my father's house" (v. 15).

No ego is involved here. There is no arrogance, unfortunately a characteristic of some great religious leaders. He actually tells God that he, Gideon, is probably the wrong choice.God responds to humility and loves the humble. The

Bible says, "And the Lord said unto him, Surely I will be with thee, and thou shalt smite the Midianites as one man" (v. 16).

In addition to his humility, we find in Gideon, a young man who wanted to be sure of his actions. There is no rashness in Gideon. He asks of the angel a sign from the Lord to show if he has found favor in God's sight.

Gideon brought the meat of a sacrificial goat, together with the broth and some unleavened cakes of bread.

He Was Willing.

This was a great sacrifice from a hungry family, but God's favor was more important to Gideon than earthly fare. The angel then instructed Gideon to place his sacrifice on a rock, and as the angel touched the sacrifice with his staff, fire rose up out of the rock and consumed the sacrifice.

Instantly, the angel disappeared from Gideon's sight. A symbolic lesson in spiritual living can be found in Gideon's sacrifice and the happenings here.

When one brings his or her best to God and places it on the solid rock, Christ Jesus, when one is then breathed upon by the fire of the Holy Spirit, whatever is brought becomes an acceptable offering to the Lord, just as Gideon's sacrifice was accepted.

Gideon named the place, "Jehovah-Shalom" (v. 24), which means "The Lord Our Peace." An altar to God was built to commemorate the place where God began this deliverance for His people.

He Was Pro-Active.

Realizing that only complete devotion to God would bring deliverance from the Midianites, Gideon obeyed God's command to tear down Baal's altars and cut down the groves of trees they had dedicated to idol gods (see vv. 25-32).

Since disobedience got Israel into this place of destitution, Gideon would do nothing except what God commanded.

In fact Gideon may be one of the most cautious men in Scripture. His cautious nature was not due to a lack of courage, but rather to a complete and full desire to be obedient and pleasing to God.

About this time the Midianites, the Amalekites, and all of "the children of the east" converged on the valley of Jezreel (v. 33).

The Bible says that the invading armies were like "grasshoppers for multitude; and their camels were without number, as the sand by the seaside for multitude" (7:12). This was a frightening site for Israel. A military mobilization threatening them like this one looming on the horizon meant nothing less than the forthcoming annihilation of Israel.

He Was Spirit-led.

In the midst of this frightening development, the Bible says that "The Spirit of the Lord came upon Gideon, and he blew a trumpet" (6:34). Quickly, the people of Abiezar, Manasseh, Asher, Zebulun and Naphtali gathered together to follow Gideon into battle.

Approximately 32,000 people responded to the trumpet call for help. This number represented a considerable army. They bivouacked at a place called "the well of Harod" (7:1). The word *Harod* means trembling, which was an apt description of most of Gideon's army.

Once again Gideon, in cautious manner, tested the Lord to be sure of His favor. He placed a fleece of wool on the ground and asked God to let the morning dew be upon the fleece only and the ground around it to be dry, if indeed God is going to use him to deliver Israel.

On the following morning Gideon was able to wring a bowl of water from the thoroughly wet fleece and the ground was dry. Then Gideon asked God to prove himself one more time. This time the fleece would be dry and the ground was to be wet with dew. God did exactly as Gideon asked (see

6:35-40). One begins to wonder how long God will tolerate this kind of bold behavior, but we must realize that this behavior was inspired more by cautious faith than it was by doubt.

Gideon believed God, yet he had to lead people into battle who doubted themselves and who had been disobedient to God for years. These tests were so contrary to natural laws, that no one could doubt that God was with Gideon.

God's Methods

Now the testing of Gideon began. God had proven *Himself*, now Gideon would have to prove *himself*. This is always true in God's dealing with us. God provides the power, but we are the instruments of that power.

In Judges 7:2, 3, God told Gideon that his army was too large. God knew the nature of the people, so He told Gideon,

> The people that are with thee are too many for me to give the Midianites into their hands, lest Israel vaunt themselves against me, saying, Mine own hand hath saved me (v. 2).

God's test for these people was very simple. He instructed Gideon to simply tell all who were afraid to go home. Twenty-two thousand — more than two thirds of his army — left immediately. Perhaps a lot could be said about cowardice here, but the chief concern of this story should be commitment.

To be afraid is a trait of human nature, but commitment overcomes cowardice. Twenty-two thousand just didn't have enough commitment for the battle.

Nor did they have the commitment to receive victory. Reception takes commitment, too; for in receiving, we assume responsibility for what we have received.

This mass exodus of uncommitted cowards left Gideon with 10,000 troops. God tells him the number is still too great for the Lord's miracle. No one would receive glory for this victory but God.

The Lord told Gideon to take them to the water and He would "try" them for Gideon; He would separate His army.

God's method was simple. Those who "lapped" water like a dog were put in a separate group. Those who knelt and drank were placed in another group. The final numbers showed 300 men who lapped like a dog, and 9,700 who knelt on their knees to drink.

God chose the 300. He said, "By the three hundred men that lapped will I save you" (v. 7).

Some have tried to spiritualize this test, seeing character traits in "lapping" or "kneeling," but it makes better sense to understand that God knows what is in every man's heart. God knew each and every person in the army and knew which 300 of the original 32,000 He could trust to carry out His plan.

Why He made them "lap as a dog" only God knows; but be that as it may, He did choose His army and pronounced them as Israel's deliverers.

Vital Elements

Gideon and his servant, Phurah, would perform one more act before they went into battle. That night they entered the camp of Midian at God's command, and listened.

Here we pause and realize the value of listening. Our propensity to talk more than listen often hampers our spiritual journeys with God. The old adage that "God gave us two ears and one mouth so we would listen twice as much as we talk" is apropos for most of us.

That night Gideon and Phurah heard two Midianite soldiers talking (see vv. 9-15). One related a dream he had to his friend. He told of seeing a huge cake of barley bread roll off the hill and obliterate the hosts of Midian.

His partner told him, "This is nothing else save the sword of Gideon . . . for into his hand hath God delivered Midian, and all the host" (v. 14).

The Bible says that when Gideon heard this, "he worshiped" (v. 15). Who can blame him? To hear this kind of confirmation from one's enemy was an extreme faith booster.

Gideon's battle plan was simplistic, but it was powerfully symbolic of God's power. He divided his army into three companies of 100 men.

- ✓ Each man was given a torch or "lamp," which was then placed in a clay pitcher where it would smolder but remain hot.

- ✓ Each man was given a trumpet. They surrounded the camp of Midian.

- ✓ When Gideon blew his trumpet, all of them were to follow his example. They would break their pitchers, and the resulting inrush of oxygen would cause the torches to flare into flames of fire.

- ✓ With a loud voice all would shout, "The sword of the Lord, and of Gideon" (see vv. 16-18).

Imagine! In the darkest hour of the night 301 torches blazed; 301 trumpets blared and 301 voices of faith and victory cried in unison, "The sword of the Lord and of Gideon!"

Complete Victory

The effect was cataclysmic. The Midianites ran in all directions, and Israel slew them to the borders of their homeland. They even slew their kings, Oreb and Zeeb (v. 25).

Notice the spiritual symbolism in Gideon's victory. A torch was kept lit until it was time to shine. A trumpet of victory was blown to announce the battle, and God's sword was declared to be the first weapon in battle.

Naturally, the people decided that Gideon should rule in Israel. He had rallied the people and had led the victory. In 8:22 the Bible says, "Then the men of Israel said unto Gideon, Rule thou over us, both thou, and thy son, and thy son's son also: for thou has delivered us from the hand of Midian."

Gideon's answer to them is a classic in Scripture, "And Gideon said unto them, I will not rule over you, neither shall my son rule over you: the Lord shall rule over you" (Judges 8:23).

Gideon retained his humility after the great victory. The recognition of God's rulership is paramount in a character of greatness.

God is sovereign and only those who recognize this fact can ever be truly great.

Time is filled with swift transition,
Naught of earth unmoved can stand,
Build your hopes on things eternal,
Hold to God's unchanging hand!

Hold to God's unchanging hand!
Hold to God's unchanging hand!
Build your hopes on things eternal,
Hold to God's unchanging hand!

– Jennie Wilson

Gideon:
The Sword of the Lord

And what shall I more say? for the time would fail me to tell of Gedeon   (Hebrews 11:32)

INTRODUCTION

When Gideon first appears on the Biblical scene, he is the most unlikely of heroic characters. In fact, we first see him as a poor, frustrated farm boy suffering from a total lack of self-esteem. His homeland was in ruins and under siege by a powerful militarized nation. Poverty and hunger ruled the land. Gideon's people — God's people, the children of Israel — were hiding like frightened animals in caves and dens in the rocks.

But God has always made much of little. He confounds the wise with the foolish, and brings down the strong with the weak. Gideon was perfect clay for the master Potter, and victory was on the way.

I. ISRAEL'S DILEMMA WAS GOD'S OPPORTUNITY.

A. Israel would be delivered for their repentance (*Judges 6:7-10*).

Outline

B. He chooses Gideon a poor farm boy to lead this deliverance (*Judges 6:12*).

C. God's presence with him would be the key to his mighty deliverance (*Judges 6:16*).

II. GIDEON'S QUALITIES WERE GOD'S TOOLS.

A. Gideon was humble (*Judges 6:15*).

B. Gideon was prayerful (*Judges 6:24*).

C. Gideon was willing (*Judges 6:27*).

D. Gideon was a man of action (*Judges 6:29*).

E. Gideon operated in the power of the Spirit (*Judges 6:34*).

III. ONLY GOD'S METHODS BRING GOD'S RESULTS.

A. God would not deliver through the power of numbers.

   1. Thirty-two thousand gathered to fight Midian (*Judges 7:3*).

   2. Twenty-two thousand of them were cowards (*Judges 7:3*).

B. God alone is worthy of glory for His work.

C. He knew people would take the credit if a large army of Israelites defeated Midian (*Judges 7:2*).

D. Twice he cut down the size of Gideon's army (*Judges 7:3-6*).

C. God chose a number of men so small, only He would be praised for this victory (*Judges 7:7*).

Outline

IV. THREE ELEMENTS IN VICTORY

  A. A trumpet, the call to battle (*Judges 7:20*)

  B. A torch, the light of battle (*Judges 7:20*)

  C. A cry, the Word in battle (*Judges 7:20*)

V. GOD'S VICTORY FOR US IS ALWAYS A COMPLETE VICTORY

  A. The trumpet is a signal that things have changed (*Joel 2:1*). The prophet Joel states that Zion (the church) should sound the alarm that things have changed and the Day of the Lord is near.

  B. A torch lights the way in battle. We are to be a torch for Christ who said, "Ye are the light of the world" (*Matthew 5:14*).

  C. A cry for the Word of God is paramount to every victory. It is the two-edged sword that completes our every triumph (*Hebrews 4:12*).

  D. Gideon's victory over Midian was complete . . . even to the extermination of Midian's Kings, Oreb and Zeeb (see Judges 7:25). God doesn't just want our life to merely be victorious; He wants it to be abundant (*John 10:10*).

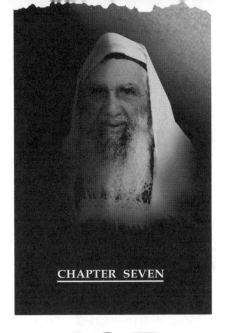

CHAPTER SEVEN

JOB
Abused But Not
Confused

*Hast thou considered my servant Job, that there is none
like him in the earth . . . ?* (Job 1:8).

THE BOOK OF JOB IS THE WONDERFUL STORY of a godly
and upright man. But Satan is convinced that once
he attacks Job and all that pertains to him, the
righteous man will deteriorate into corruption.

Job has the complete confidence of the Almighty,
however. God even boasts of Job's righteousness
and holds him up as an example of perfection. The

ensuing onslaught on Job and the eternal question of "Why do the righteous suffer?" fills this book with intrigue and gives heavenly comfort to all generations who find themselves in similar dilemmas.

EARTHLY AND SPIRITUAL PROSPERITY

Job was a wealthy man. Among nomadic peoples, wealth was measured primarily in the size of their herds and in the number of their servants. The Bible records that Job owned

- ✓ 7,000 sheep,
- ✓ 3,000 camels,
- ✓ 500 yoke of oxen,
- ✓ 500 donkeys, and
- ✓ a great number of servants.

He is labeled "the greatest of all the men of the east" (Job 1:3). But to the spiritually observant, Job's abundance of riches is measured best in the depths of his character. The Bible uses the words "perfect" and "upright" to describe him. He is said to have "feared God" and "hated evil," the first of these characteristics naturally producing the other.

Job was a dedicated family man, who was father to seven sons and three daughters. Job was very concerned about the eternal and spiritual welfare of his family, for the Bible said he continually "sanctified them" and offered up burnt offerings in their behalf before God (v. 5).

Thus, Job spent his life living in prosperity, an astute business man, yet with a keen sense of duty as a father and as priest of his home. His lifestyle is an example for God's people in all generations.

It is not enough to be successful in earthly endeavors if we are not successful in spiritual ones.

When we are successful in spiritual matters, we have a moral and Biblical obligation to go before God in behalf of our families. The family is an institution ordained of God with specific structure dictated by Scripture. Job took his role as priest of his home with the utmost seriousness.

So do all of God's true servants.

- ✓ Abraham's devotion was passed to Isaac, and it saved his nephew Lot from the tragedy of Sodom.
- ✓ Timothy possessed the "unfeigned faith" of his mother Lois and his grandmother, Eunice (2 Timothy 1:5).
- ✓ Joshua was bold in his declaration, "But as for me and my house, we will serve the Lord" (Joshua 24:15).

Job's greatest treasure was his faith in God and in God's sovereignty. He exercised his faith with his family continually, making Job the wealthiest of men.

ACCUSATIONS AND APPROVAL

The story of Job begins to unfold with a conversation between God and Satan that takes place in heaven (see Job 1:6-12). God boasts of Job's integrity and righteousness to Satan, who retaliates with the answer, "Doth Job fear God for nought?" (v. 9).

Satan, the accuser, then insinuates that Job serves God only because of his material blessings and the hedge of protection God has built around him (v. 10).

Satan challenged Job's integrity further by asking God to take the down the hedge around him and let him destroy all that Job has. Satan's assumption is verbalized to God, "And he will curse thee to thy face" (v. 11).

Here Satan is seen best in his role as the accuser of the brethren. That he has the arrogance and pride in his own ability to discourage the saints and to make this accusation before God shows a remarkable amount of self-confidence. God knows the score, however; and God knew His servant Job.

This is also a powerful picture of God's confidence in His children. It is a portrait of the

Almighty's superiority over Satan. God releases Job to the devil's onslaught, but doesn't allow Satan to touch him personally (see v. 12). God is still very much in control of the situation.

Satan, bent on Job's destruction, leaves the presence of God and begins what he thinks will be Job's demise. As this story unfolds, it is a comfort to realize that God recognizes the power of our faith. He knows the stalwart nature of godly character, and the extent it can endure.

Job is not thrown helplessly to the wolves; instead, he is bolstered by a fortress of faith that has been years in the making. His character is as solid as Gibraltar's rock, and hurricane-force winds from hell's legions cannot erode what God has built.

The first thing Satan does in his abusive attack on Job is to destroy his earthly wealth. Satan's prideful nature assumes that Job's peace lies in the abundance of things he possesses.

Sabeans come and steal his oxen and donkeys; they slay the plowman and herdsmen that attend them. While Job is receiving this report from an escaping messenger, he learns that a "fire" has fallen from heaven and consumed his 7,000 sheep and the shepherds who tended them. The original Hebrew here denotes "A fierce lightning from heaven" which indicates that Satan, the prince and power of the air, was viciously at work. The fact that the Bible uses the phrase "of God" indicates the permission of God for this disaster in verse 16.

TRIUMPH IN ADVERSITY

Throughout these calamities the Bible uses the phrase, "While he was yet speaking," indicating that all events took place one after the other. As soon as Job learns of the disaster of his flocks of sheep, another messenger tells him of an attack by the Chaldeans on his camels and camel tenders. All 3,000 camels were stolen, and the tenders were slain.

Such a herd of camels indicates that Job was in the caravan trade, a profitable enterprise in the ancient Middle East. This aspect of his wealth is now bankrupt. The bells jingling on the bridles of Job's huge camel trains would be heard no more.

In a moment's time, Job has gone from a wealthy magnate to a penniless pauper. His wealth is consumed by the disasters of a few moments. Poverty and deprivation loom before him. And while he contemplates this calamity, the worst fear any man can realize in the flesh becomes a reality. A messenger more forlorn than all the rest arrives. One can imagine the impact of his message: it is a tale of ultimate tragedy.

Job's seven sons and three daughters were enjoying a feast at the eldest brother's home. A horrible cyclonic wind arose. Its circular motion smote the four corners of the house in which they were feasting. The house collapsed, killing all inside! This trembling servant is the only survivor of this calamity of horror.

Job was a father. He was a loving, caring, giving, praying father. He had seen these 10 children as wet, wrinkled newborns. He had delighted in them as waddling toddlers. He had watched them grow and mature, and develop into adults. Now . . . in a whisper . . . they were all gone.

Not only was he an instant pauper, he was now childless. All that the world views as signs of prosperity was gone. What would be Job's reaction to life's supreme abuse? Can we fathom his feelings of helplessness? What does one say in a moment like this?

Job's reaction defies human reason. It can only be understood under the microscope of faith. The Bible says it best,

> Then Job arose, and rent his mantle, and shaved his head, and fell down upon the ground, and worshiped, And said, Naked came I out of my mother's womb, and naked shall I return thither: the Lord gave, and the Lord hath taken away; blessed be the name of

the Lord. In all this Job sinneth not, nor charged God foolishly (vv. 20-22).

Job's reaction is a brilliant exhibition of faith in action. His nine points of contrition are noteworthy:

1. Job humbled himself—He "rent his mantle, shaved his head, and fell down."

2. Job worshiped God—"and worshiped."

3. He acknowledged how he came into being—"Naked came I out of my mother's womb."

4. He understood how he would leave this life—"And naked shall I return thither."

5. He acknowledged the source of all blessings—"The Lord gave."

6. He understood God's sovereignty—"The Lord hath taken away."

7. He knew that God was worthy of praise in spite of his own personal losses—"Blessed be the name of the Lord."

8. He refused to backslide—"In all this Job sinned not."

9. He was not foolish enough to blame God—"Nor charged God foolishly."

Job passed the test! He had not crumbled as Satan indicated he would. He would not curse God.

Job was all God said he was. He had proven himself "perfect and upright" in the midst of unthinkable adversity. Yet, Job's testing had only begun.

So it is true in life. We never are free from life's misfortunes. One challenge in life is followed quickly by another. A believer can never be so lax in this life that he or she assume all trials, valleys and battles are past.

The Bible is clear in its message of warning and comfort, "Many are the afflictions of the righteous: but the Lord delivereth him out of them all" (Psalm 34:19). Our troubles are many, but we are delivered out of all our troubles. Our afflictions are innumerable but we are delivered from all of them. One valley follows another, but God is with us.

Battlefields are all around us, but the battle is the Lord's (see 1 Samuel 17:47). Sin abounds, but grace much more abounds (see Romans 5:20).

As it was in the life of God's servant, Job, so it is in the life of every believer. He who calmed the storm says, "I will never leave nor forsake you" (see Hebrews 13:5). Job's trials were to be more severe, but the grace of Job's God would also be more than sufficient.

After Job's triumph of worship following his first trial, the Bible records another meeting that took place in the presence of God. Satan tells God of his wandering the length and breadth of the earth.

Again, God boasts of Job's integrity, this time reminding Satan that Job has remained steadfast in his character, despite all his losses. Satan counters with the accusation that men may lose *things*, but they break when they themselves are attacked in their physical person.

He then asks the Almighty to allow him to afflict Job physically. Satan declares emphatically that this time Job will indeed "curse thee to thy face" (see Job 2:1-5).

The sovereign God of heaven and earth did not hesitate to allow Satan this freedom. Once again, it indicated that God knew the depth of Job's character. He places one restriction on Satan, however; Satan cannot touch Job's life.

What comfort to know that God has the final say as to whether we live or die! Hebrews 9:27 is plain, "It is appointed unto men once to die, but after this the judgement." Death is an appointed matter, and who but the Giver of life has the right to determine when it shall end?

PERSONAL ATTACK

God's boundaries on Satan concerning Job are not only justified, they are a matter of divine prerogative. God has always had power over Satan, and He always will have power over Satan!

So Satan attacked Job's body. He was covered with festering boils from "the sole of his foot unto his crown" (Job 2:7). The itching was unbearable. He sat in soft ashes for relief, and scratched himself with a broken piece of pottery.

The disease progressed. His gums swelled until the distortion made his speech sound like the roaring of an animal.

- ✓ In 3:24 he said, "My roarings are poured out like the waters."
- ✓ He became emaciated and wasted. He was little more than skin stretched over skeleton. He was abhorrent to behold.
- ✓ He cried, "My flesh is clothed with worms and clods of dust; my skin is broken, and become loathsome" (7:5).
- ✓ He weeps and says, "My face is foul with weeping and my eyelids is the shadow of death" (16:16).
- ✓ In 17:1 he says, "My breath is corrupt, my days are extinct, the graves are ready for me."
- ✓ Listen to his cry of anguish, "My bone cleaveth to my skin and to my flesh, and I am escaped with the skin of my teeth" (19:20).

In the midst of this horrible sickness and disfigurement, Job was troubled with problems from people. He tells how little children despise him (19:18) and how his kinsfolk let him down (v. 14). His own servants avoided him (v. 16) and friends forgot him (v. 14).

Much of the Book of Job deals with how his three best friends — Eliphaz, Bildad and Zophar — wailed at the sight of him and began to question his integrity. Their arguments were based on the premise that the righteous don't suffer. Indeed, if they did God would seem to be unjust, they said.

Then the greatest of all disappointments beset Job. His wife, who had been with him in the loss of their children and who had remained steadfast as the possessions disappeared, now turns on him when she sees this wasted, sickened man.

In 2:9 the Bible records, "Then said his wife unto him, Dost thou still retain thine integrity? Curse God and die." What betrayal! How could the one who was one flesh with him so despise and disdain him?

Job's answer to her is justification for God's confidence in him. "But he said unto her, Thou speakest as one of the foolish women speaketh. What? Shall we receive good at the hand of God, and shall we not receive evil? In all this did not Job sin with his lips" (v. 10). Here is unfeigned, unshakable faith in God! Facing out-of-control circumstances he remains in control of his own character.

He is not superhuman. Discouragement and misery were constant companions, and his friends sought tenaciously to find some reason or fault in him that would explain his suffering. They earned the facetious nickname, "Job's Comforters."

- ✓ In 4:1-11, Eliphaz the Temanite told him he had reaped what he had sown.

- ✓ In 8:3-22, Bildad the Shuhite accused Job of hypocrisy and his children of great sins.

- ✓ In 11:1-4, Zophar the Naamathite accuses Job of five sins: (1) talking too much; (2) self-justification; (3) lying; (4) mocking and (5) false claims. Job answered his accusers one by one and remained patient and steadfast.

TESTIMONY JUSTIFIES FAITH

During his suffering Job made two of the most famous and powerful statements of faith in the Bible.

The first one is found in 13:25, "Though he slay me, yet will I trust in him." This cry of confidence in God from a dying man shows that the threat of death did not erode Job's faith and trust in the God he loved.

The second statement of faith is found in 19:23-27:

Oh that my words were now written! Oh that they were printed in a book! That they were

———

graven with an iron pen and lead in the rock forever! For I know that my redeemer liveth, and that he shall stand at the latter day upon the earth: And though after my skin worms destroy this body, yet in my flesh shall I see God: Whom I shall see for myself, and mine eyes shall behold, and not another; though my reins be consumed within me (19:23-27).

FAITHFULNESS IS REWARDED

In this holy proclamation, Job's testimony became a prophecy of the resurrection. This patriarch and saint became a prophet of renown while wasting away on an ash heap.

His Redeemer *did* live; his Redeemer *would* stand at the latter day upon the earth. He *would* see God as a living soul, alive for all eternity. What hope these words have given men and women through the ages! How many times have they been read at grave sites around the world, while hope leaped in the hearts of the living?

But enough is enough and all things must eventually come to an end. One day, God heard Job praying for his friends, and said, "That's enough." The Bible says, "The Lord turned the captivity of Job, when he prayed for his friends" (42:10). God blessed the latter days of Job's life more than his former years. In fact, God "gave Job twice as much as he had before" (v. 10).

The second time around Job was given 14,000 sheep, 6,000 camels, 1,000 yoke of oxen and 1,000 donkeys.

God also gave him, in due time, seven sons and three daughters. The scriptures state that no women in the land were so fair as the daughters of Job, and Job gave them an inheritance among their brethren (v. 15).

After all this, Job lived 140 more years and saw his descendants to four generations. The original Hebrew says that "Job died being satisfied with his life" (v. 17). The Septuagint adds the following words to this verse, "And it is written that he shall rise again with those whom the Lord raises up."

So lived and died a saint of God. He was certainly abused, but never confused!

I care not today the morrow may bring;
If shadow or sunshine or rain.
The Lord I know ruleth o'er everything,
And all of my worry is vain.

– James Wells

Job, Abused But Not Confused

Hast thou considered my servant Job, that there is none like him in the earth. . . ? (Job 1:8).

INTRODUCTION

The Book of Job is the wonderful story of a godly and upright man. Satan was convinced that Job would deteriorate into corruption once he and all that pertained to him was attacked. Job had the complete confidence of the Almighty, however. God boasted of Job's righteousness and held him up as an example of perfection.

The ensuing onslaught on Job and the eternal question, "Why do the righteous suffer?" fill this book with intrigue and gives heavenly comfort for all generations who find themselves in like dilemmas.

I. JOB HAD EARTHLY AND SPIRITUAL PROSPERITY.

A. Job was wealthy in stock and, apparently, the caravan and commerce industries (*Job 1:3*)

1. 7,000 sheep for wool and clothing

2. 3,000 camels in the caravan trade

3. 500 yoke of oxen for farming and agriculture

4. 500 donkeys used in commerce

B. Job had a fine family.
  1. Job had seven sons and three daughters (*Job 1:2*).
  2. Job offered prayer for them continually (*Job 1:5*).
  3. Job was perfect and upright, hating evil (*Job 1:1*).

II. GOD'S APPROVAL AND SATAN'S ACCUSATIONS

A. A meeting in heaven (*Job 1:6*).

B. God boasts of Job as His servant (*Job 1:8*).

C. Satan accuses Job of serving for divine favor and blessing (*Job 1:9-10*).

D. God releases Satan to attack Job's possessions to prove Job's devotion to God (*Job 1:12*).

III. JOB'S TRIUMPH IN ADVERSITY

A. Satan destroys Job's possessions (*Job 1:13-17*).

B. Satan destroys Job's family (*Job 1:18-19*).

C. Job's response of worship acknowledges God's sovereignty in his life (*Job 1:20-22*).

IV. THE ATTACK ON JOB'S PERSON

A. Satan, rebuffed by Job's integrity, asks God for permission to destroy his body. Permission is granted with limitations (*Job 2:1-6*).

B. Job is attacked physically in a horrible fashion (*Job 2:7, 8; 7:5; 16:16; 17:1; 19:20*).

Outline

C. The human race attacks Job; people let him down.
1. His wife (*Job 2:9*)
2. His best friends: Eliphaz, Bildad and Zophar (*Job 4:1-11; 8:3-22; 11:1-4*)
3. Plus children, servants and kinsfolk (*Job 19:14-18*)

V. JOB'S TESTIMONY JUSTIFIES FAITH (Matthew 12:37)

A. He testifies of God's sovereignty (*Job 13:15*).

B. He testifies of eternal life (*Job 19:23-27*).

C. He testifies through his prayer for his accusers (*Job 42:10*).

D. He prophecies of Christ (*Job 19:25*).

VI. JOB'S FAITHFULNESS REWARDED

A. God restored and doubled his possessions (*Job 42:12*).

B. God restored his family (*Job 42:13*).

C. God blessed him with a long and happy life (*Job 42:16, 17*).

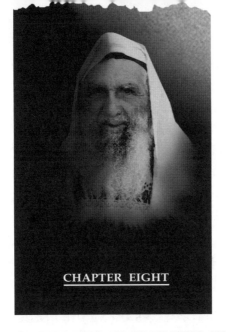

CHAPTER EIGHT

EZEKIEL

Strange Man of God

The word of the Lord came expressly unto Ezekiel the priest, the son of Buzi, in the land of the Chaldeans by the river Chebar; and the hand of the Lord was there upon him (Ezekiel 1:3).

THE BOOK OF THE EZEKIEL WAS WRITTEN WHILE EZEKIEL was in Babylonian captivity, sometime between 622 and 600 B.C.

Inspired powerfully by the Holy Spirit, the prophet Ezekiel received an extraordinary number of direct revelations, which he imparted to his people. Many are in pantomime: of the 40 pantomimes listed in scripture, 25 are in the Book of Ezekiel.

A FOURFOLD PROPHECY

As we shall see, Ezekiel was a most unusual servant of God and perhaps the most unflinchingly obedient man in Scripture. His prophecies are of four general types.

First, he prophesied of the immediate captivity of Israel, and of certain impending doom including the destruction of Jerusalem.

Secondly, he prophesied against other nations for their influence on the sins and iniquities of Israel.

Thirdly, he prophesied of Israel in the last days, just prior to the return of the Messiah. He foretold of the unspeakable judgements God would pour out on the wicked.

Finally, Ezekiel prophesied of the millennial temple and the glorious reign of the Messiah over Israel.

A short treatise such as this cannot do justice to the Book of Ezekiel, or to the many intricate details of his prophecy. However, a look at the character of this Jewish prophet/priest provides a portrait of a man totally sold out to God.

In Ezekiel, we see a character of such depth of devotion, that for the sake of the God and the people he loved, he cast aside popular opinion of himself and unashamedly exposed his life to ridicule. He did this in order to bring redemption to others.

What character! Can we discern such a man and understand what motivates him? Sadly, our hour is lacking in spiritual giants like Ezekiel. The spiritual battlefield of our day sees a wounded church infatuated with materialism, looking for selfless heroes of the faith who will lead the straying back to a loving God.

✓ We have plenty of devils, but we have a shortage of harpists like David to drive them away.

✓ Where are the pools of tears left by sobbing Jeremiahs?

✓ How long has it been since we viewed the headless body of a spiritual Goliath as we "chased" the enemy?

✓ When was the last time we heard the roaring crumble of Jericho's walls and shouted . . . for the Lord had given us the city?

✓ Do we sing and praise God at midnight anymore, while our stocks and chains are shattered and jailers beg for a place to repent?

✓ Are we willing to leave the grandeur and hoopla of a city-wide revival and journey to a desert where one poor Ethiopian needs to understand that Jesus is the subject of Isaiah 53?

Ezekiel was the strange and unusual man whom God's people needed in such an hour. Focus on him as he is depicted in God's Word and you will raise an eyebrow more than once. The only place to start studying Ezekiel is at the beginning.

A FREE CAPTIVE

When the book opens, we find Ezekiel in captivity beside a river named Chebar in the land of Babylon. The last words of Ezekiel 1:3 provide a powerful commentary on this captive priest: "And the hand of the Lord was there upon him."

Forget the chains and shackles. The loneliness of a foreign land meant nothing, for the hand of the God who measures the heavens and holds the waters was upon His servant Ezekiel. That made all the difference.

Depression becomes elation when God's hand is upon you. Distress is changed to delight when He places His mighty hand upon you. David the King, had prophesied of Israel's Babylonian captivity and had painted a very forlorn picture.

In Psalm 137:1-4, the Bible records a sad story:

> By the rivers of Babylon, there we sat down, yea, we wept when we remembered Zion. We hanged our harps upon the willows in the midst thereof. For there they that carried us away captive required of us a song; and they

that wasted us required of us mirth, saying, Sing us one of the songs of Zion. How shall we sing the Lord's song in a strange land?

Ezekiel was in captivity. He was an Israelite priest. He was beside a river in Babylon, just as David had prophesied. But Ezekiel was different than the other captives.

Ezekiel had the hand of the Lord upon him. This caused many things to happen in his life and his demeanor was different from what one would expect of a captive.

A VISION OF CHRIST

In Ezekiel 1:4, He begins to describe a time of heaven opening up to him and the visions of God that he saw. He saw four living creatures in Ezekiel 1:5 and, in Ezekiel 1:10. He described the face that each creature had.

The faces were of a man, a lion, an ox and an eagle. It is noteworthy to stop here and be reminded that each of these faces represents a side of the Messiah, Christ Jesus.

✓ As a lion is used in scripture to denote Kingship, so Christ was the "Lion of the tribe of Judah," the King of all kings.

✓ Jesus was a man, God in the flesh.

✓ An ox is a lowly and humble servant, and the ox reminds us of Jesus the servant who "came not to be ministered unto, but to minister, and to give His life a ransom for many" (Matthew 20:28).

✓ The last face Ezekiel saw was that of an eagle. An eagle is the most highly lifted up of all God's creatures, and indeed, Christ was highly exalted and lifted up (Philippians 2:9).

Ezekiel also beheld fire, lightning and brightness in this vision, denoting that what he saw was a work of the Spirit of God. The vision was circular, and Ezekiel described it as a "wheel in the middle of a wheel" (Ezekiel 1:16).

He saw the firmament, a rainbow, and a "Likeness of a throne" (Ezekiel 1:22-28). He summed it up by saying, "This was the appearance of the likeness of the glory of the Lord" (Ezekiel 1:28).

And from this vision God spoke to Ezekiel about the sins and the rebellious nature of the people. He commanded the prophet to speak God's words to them. All of this was written upon a scroll, which gives us Ezekiel's first strange act of obedience.

Ezekiel was commanded to eat the scroll (Ezekiel 3:1). His response was swift and almost comical. "So I opened my mouth" (Ezekiel 3:2).

AN EXAMPLE OF OBEDIENCE

One thing that stands out about Ezekiel is his lack of hesitation. When God spoke, Ezekiel moved. When God commanded, Ezekiel obeyed. In an hour of debate and argument with scriptural demands, Ezekiel's attitude is very refreshing. Here was a man who believed God.

Beside a river of bondage, the heavens were opened to him. Rivers of bondage break most people. People tend to give up and grow despairingly worse in their bondage to sins, habits, lifestyles and harmful attitudes. But Ezekiel got better, not bitter. He embarked on a strange life of obedience, and God used him to teach a rebellious nation His ways.

In Ezekiel 3:26, God literally made Ezekiel "dumb" or unable to speak until God instructed him. This miracle demonstrated to the people that God was in control of Ezekiel's life and what he had to say was from God.

In Ezekiel 4:12, Ezekiel used a clay tile for an object lesson pantomime in which the tile represented, Jerusalem. Ezekiel laid siege to it, demonstrating God's impending wrath upon the city.

In Ezekiel 4:3, he placed an iron skillet upon his face to show how Jerusalem would be besieged. He was then commanded to lay upon his left side for 390 days. These days represented the number of years that the iniquity of Israel had been seen by God.

These 390 years were from the division of the Kingdom under Jeroboam and Rehoboam until the 11th year of the reign of King Zedekish when Jerusalem fell (Ezekiel 4:4, 5).

In Ezekiel 4:6, the prophet was then told to lay on his right side for 40 days. These 40 days represented 40 years of Judah's iniquity, from the 13th year of the reign of Josiah when Jeremiah began his prophecy regarding judgement of Judah and Jerusalem, through Jehoiakim and Zedekiah's reign.

What perseverance Ezekiel must have had! How trying this ordeal must have been to his body and spirit! Yet Ezekiel was possessed with a sense of mission and would not be deterred in fulfilling the commands of God.

To further illustrate his destruction of Jerusalem, God had Ezekiel take a "barber's razor" and shave his head and beard (Ezekiel 5:1). He weighed and divided the hair. Then he burned a third of it, smote a third with his knife and scattered the final third to the wind.

A small remnant on the ground was bound in his skirts, taken outside the gates of the city and burned in the fire. Thus God prophesied through him that a third of the population of Jerusalem would die of pestilence and famine. Another third would fall by the sword. The remaining third would be scattered to the four winds (Ezekiel 4:12).

Before the Book of Ezekiel ends, the prophet has:

✓ prophesied to the mountains (Ezekiel 6:1-10),

✓ made a chain (7:23-27),

✓ dug through a wall (12:1-6),

✓ ate and drank while shaking and trembling (12:17-28),

✓ put a pot of meat on to boil as an object lesson (24:1-14),

✓ lost his wife (the "desire of his eyes") by a stroke and wasn't even allowed to mourn her (24:15-27).

He also prophesied to a field of dry bones (37:1-14) and used two sticks to demonstrate God's dealings with Judah and Israel (37:15-28).

Ezekiel was a man for his times. In fact, throughout the book God refers to Ezekiel as a "son of man." Ezekiel's name means "God strengthens." There is no way Ezekiel could have done what he did without divine strength. The power of his own flesh would have failed him, but God strengthened him for every task. He was placed on this earth and raised up by God to impact the human race.

And make an impact he did! Perhaps the most poignant and powerful words of Ezekiel concern last-day prophecies and events. Chapters 37-39 of Ezekiel contain a message to humankind from God that give us much insight to last-day events and what God wants his people to know.

A LAST DAYS PROPHET

Ezekiel 37 is one of the most famous passages of scripture in the Old Testament. Here God takes Ezekiel on a spiritual journey. Both symbolically and literally, He gives the prophet one of the most powerful prophecies of all time, one that was fulfilled in the 48th year of the twentieth century.

Ezekiel begins this chapter of prophecy by stating again that "The hand of the Lord was upon me" (Ezekiel 37:la). He then says that the hand "Carried me out in the spirit of the Lord, and set me down in the midst of the valley which was full of bones" (37:1b). God questioned him, "Son of man, can these bones live?" (37:3b).

Ezekiel's answer is the classic answer of faith, "O Lord God, thou knowest" (37:3b). This answer is the testimony of Ezekiel's life. He had complete trust in the omniscience of Almighty God.

No doubts plagued the mind of Ezekiel. He was resolved to God's sovereignty and it was a healthy spiritual resolve. God doesn't mind natural human curiosity, nor does He flinch at our questioning. But when His servants reach a state of spiritual maturity in which they can resolve themselves to His goodness and sovereignty, they establish a bond with Him that allows their faith to be rewarded without interruption.

Ezekiel's faith was much like that of Abraham who asked rhetorically, "Shall not the Judge of all the earth do right?" (Genesis 18:25). Here is the same calm exclamation of faith stating, "O Lord God, thou knowest" (Ezekiel 37:3).

As Ezekiel prophecies to those bones, God breathes on this valley of bleached and calcified skulls, femurs and metacarpals. The scriptures say that a noise was heard. The noise was accompanied by a shaking the bones came together in their divinely-assigned position.

This army of skeletons was quickly covered with sinew, flesh and skin. Ezekiel is commanded to prophecy to the four winds, and it is here that once again we notice a phrase that is seen throughout the Book of Ezekiel, "So I prophecied as I was commanded" (37:7; 37:10).

Ezekiel's life was one of pure obedience. Is it ridiculous to the mortal eye for a man to prophesy to scattered bones and lifeless corpses? Of course. It defies the rules of reality recognized by human culture.

But God's ways are never man's ways and Ezekiel was God's servant. He was keenly aware that God's methods get God's results. As he prophesied, breath came into those corpses and they stood on their feet, "an exceeding great army" (37:10).

God explained to Ezekiel in 37:11-28 that the bones represented Israel, scattered as a people to the four corners of the earth. They were no longer a nation, but forlornly cried "Our bones are dried, and our hope is lost: we are cut off for our parts" (37:11).

Of course, this was the case after the year A.D. 70 when Titus, the Roman General, besieged and ransacked Jerusalem. Josephus, the first-century Jewish historian, relates that the Romans so devastated the city that they tore the temple down completely and plowed the ground where it stood with teams of oxen.

Jesus himself prophesied that "Jerusalem shall be trodden down of the Gentiles, until the times of the Gentiles be fulfilled," and that the nation itself would be "led away captive into all nations" (Luke 21:24).

History proved both Ezekiel and Jesus to be correct. For 1,900 years, Israel did not exist as a nation. The descendents of Abraham, Isaac and Jacob were scattered to the far-flung regions of the earth. The despot Adolph Hitler butchered and annihilated 6 million of them in the death camps of the Third Reich.

But the desolation was not to last forever. A captive prophet named Ezekiel was told by the Almighty that though divided as two nations (Judah and Israel) and scattered as a people, He would unite them as one and bring them back to the land He promised Abraham (see Ezekiel 37:22).

At the end of World War II, thousands of homeless Jews began to converge on the land of Palestine. God began to work through the two most powerful nations on earth, the United States and Great Britain. After much debate and discussion, as well as concessions and treaties, the nation of Israel was formed in 1948.

It happened in one day as Isaiah had prophesied, "Who hath heard such a thing? who hath seen such things? Shall the earth be made to bring forth in one day? or shall a nation be born at once? for as soon as Zion travailed, she brought forth her children" (Isaiah 66:8).

Zion had travailed at Dachau, Auschwitz and Belsen. The bones of God's people had been bleached in Nazi genocide. For hundreds of years, persecution had spread the people of Israel throughout the earth, but the prophecy God gave through His servant Ezekiel would come to pass. God's Word is immutable.

Ezekiel 38 and 39 foretells a time when certain nations to the far north of Israel—along with their allies from Persia (Iraq and Iran), Ethiopia and Libya—would come against Israel in a united front to destroy her.

In Ezekiel 38:2, God tells the prophet that the descendents of Magog, Meschech and Tubal will be allied against Israel in the last days. Magog, Meschech and Tubal were the sons of Japheth, Noah's third son. Japheth's son, Gomer, is also mentioned in Ezekiel 38:6 as one of these allies.

These sons of Japheth are the ancestors of the Scythians, Russians, Muscovites, Tibereni, Cappadocians and other peoples who predominate in northern Europe and Asia. It is interesting to note that many of these make up the southern tier of the former Soviet Union.

Together with their allies, they are today predominately Muslim and fiercely anti-Semitic. The thrust of this prophecy is that in "the latter years" these nations will attack Israel and when they do, God will destroy them (see 38:8-16). The details are many, but the main idea contained in this prophecy is that this battle is a latter-day event.

The fact that Israel will take seven years to clean up the battlefield with fire indicates that this battle may take place about the time of the rapture of the church. According to 39:11, this will be known as the battle of Hamongog, and it will take seven full months to bury the dead. God will be glorified by Israel for this victory (39:13).

The prophecies of Ezekiel 37 through 39 are of such importance that volumes could be written on each chapter and their fulfillment.

To understand the man Ezekiel, it is important to grasp the fact that here was a man with a godly conscience where history was concerned. He believed that God was the divine architect over the affairs of the earth, and that man was made to glorify Him.

He understood that Israel, Jacob's children, were God's chosen people. He understood that God had a plan for them in the process of world redemption. Ezekiel was willing and obedient even if it meant personal ridicule and judgement foretold on his own people.

SOVEREIGN OVER ETERNITY

The last four words written by Ezekiel are a wonderful summation of what God was saying through him. He prophesies of the eternal New Jerusalem: "And the name of the city from that day shall be, The Lord is there" (Ezekiel 48:35).

What a wonderful word from God! What a perfect name for the city of God, "Adonai-shammah" — the Lord is there.

May we, like Ezekiel, pray for redemption to come, and for sin to be eradicated. Then when we reach our city of delight, we will approach the gates with praise for "the Lord is there."

If I walk in the pathway of duty,
If I work till the close of the day,
I shall see the great King in His beauty,
When I've gone the last mile of the way.

When I've gone the last mile of the way,
I will rest at the close of the day,
And I know there are joys that await me,
When I've gone the last mile of the way.

– Johnson Oatman, Jr.

Ezekiel, Strange Man of God

The word of the Lord came expressly unto Ezekiel the priest, the son of Buzi, in the land of the Chaldeans by the river Chebar; and the hand of the Lord was there upon him (Ezekiel 1:3).

INTRODUCTION

One of the most unusual men in the Bible is the prophet Ezekiel, whose book of prophecy is singularly unique in the Old Testament. Written between 622 and 600 B.C., while Ezekiel was a captive in Babylon, it is a book that demonstrates triumph in adversity, unflinching obedience to God and unblemished hope for the future.

Ezekiel was a master of the pantomime and object lesson and the future of our current world is made clearer because of his obedience.

I. EZEKIEL, A CAPTIVE FREE IN THE SPIRIT

A. Ezekiel was a captive beside a river in Babylon (*Ezekiel 1:3*).

1. David had prophesied of the demeanor of Israel in captivity (*Psalm 137:1-4*).

2. But Ezekiel had God's hand upon him (*1:3*).

Outline

B. Ezekiel had Heaven opened to him (*1:1*).

C. Ezekiel had his eyes on God (*1:1*).

D. He saw a vision of "the glory of the Lord" (*1:28*).

II. EZEKIEL'S BOOK IS A FOURFOLD VISION.

   A. Job prophesied of the immediate captivity of Israel and the doom of Jerusalem

   B. Job prophesied against other nations for their influence on the sins and iniquities of Israel.

   C. Job prophesied of Israel in the last days and God's judgements on the wicked.

   D. Job prophesied of a millennial temple and God's just and glorious reign over Israel

III. EZEKIEL HAD A VISION OF CHRIST (*1:5-10*).

   A. The Man: Christ was God in the flesh (*1 Timothy 3:16*).

   B. The Lion: Christ was a King (*John 18:37*).

   C. The Ox: Christ was a servant (*Matthew 20:28*, NIV).

   D. The Eagle: Christ was exalted (*Philippians 2:9*).

IV. EZEKIEL MODELED OBEDIENCE AT ALL COSTS.

   A. He obeys without hesitation (*Ezekiel 3:2*).

   B. He prophesies at God's command (*37:7*).

   C. Ezekiel's pantomimes illustrate his submission.

      1. Razor pantomime (*5:1*)

      2. Eating and drinking while trembling (*12:17-28*)

3. Not mourning at his wife's death, though he loved her dearly (24:15-27)
4. Lying on his left side 390 days and on his right side 40 days (4:4-6)

V. EZEKIEL WAS A "LAST DAYS" PROPHET.

A. *Ezekiel 37* – The dry bones and the restoration of Israel

1. Israel's scattering and hopelessness are foretold (37:11).
2. God is the author of this miracle of restoration (37:12).
3. Israel will be united and undivided as a last day nation *(37:22).*

B. *Ezekiel 38 and 39*

1. Ezekiel prophesies that Israel will be attacked in the last days by a massive army (38:9-12).
2. God says He will annihilate this attacking army (38:21-23; 39:1-7).
3. The earth will know God has wrought this victory (38:23; 39:7).

VI. EZEKIEL PROPHESIED OF GOD'S SOVEREIGNTY OVER ETERNITY

A. *Ezekiel 40-48*, a portrait of the millennial temple
B. *Ezekiel 48:35*, a summation of all things, the millennial city is called, *Adonai-shammah,* meaning "the Lord is there." God's presence is eternal.

PART II

Saints of the New Testament

Time would fail me to tell of . . . others . . . . (Of
whom the world was not worthy). . . . And these
all . . . obtained a good report through faith
(Hebrews 11:32, 36, 38, 39).

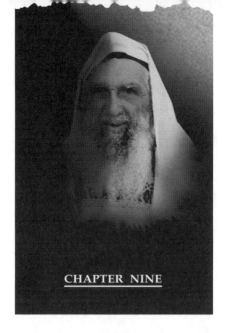

CHAPTER NINE

MATTHEW
The King Announcer

And as Jesus passed forth from thence, he saw a man, named Matthew, sitting at the receipt of custom: and he saith unto him, Follow me. And he arose, and followed him (Matthew 9:9).

FOR THE FIRST TWO CENTURIES AFTER CHRIST, Matthew's Gospel was the Gospel most frequently quoted by the early church fathers. The first of the four profound portraits of Jesus, it is noteworthy that Matthew takes special pains to establish the link between Old and New Testaments. He presents Jesus in a beautiful way—as Israel's Messiah and long-awaited King.

FOUR PORTRAITS OF CHRIST

Biographically, Matthew gives us an orderly account of Jesus' actions and teachings while he carefully intertwines these happenings as the fulfillment of Old Testament prophecy concerning the Messiah. Matthew gives us a Jesus who is King, Servant and Son of God.

Theologically, it is clear that Matthew wrote under the inspiration of the Holy Spirit to answer any questions that Jewish believers might have. An early church father, Origen, believed that this first Gospel was prepared for converts from Judaism and first published in the Hebrew tongue.

Matthew also wrote about Jesus from an *ethical standpoint.* He is telling us that Jesus came not to abolish the Law and the prophets, but to fulfill the scriptures. Jesus' words in Matthew 7:15-21 teach clearly that God is interested in the motivations of the heart. It is not so much what we do, but who we are.

Finally, Matthew's Gospel is *an evangelistic tool* of great power. He warns of judgement to come and gives detailed insight into last-day prophetic events and warnings against hypocrisy in Christ's condemnation of the Pharisees and Sadducees.

Matthew's Gospel is a complete book. Although it focuses on Matthew's dear Lord and never on the writer, this Gospel gives all of us a brief glimpse into Matthew's own character. This alone certainly deserves our study.

MATTHEW, THE DISCIPLE

In Matthew 9, Mark 2 and Luke 5, we read of the calling of Matthew. His home was in Capernaum beside the Sea of Galilee.

He was the son of a man named Alpheus (Mark 2:14), and some feel he was the brother of two other disciples, James and Thaddeus because their father's name was also Alpheus (see Matthew 10:3; Luke 6:16). Tradition says that Simon Zelotes was also their brother.

If the traditional stories are true, there were actually four sets of brothers among the disciples: Peter and Andrew; James and John, the sons of Zebedee; Philip and Nathaniel (also called Bartholomew); and the sons of Alpheus.

From this nugget of New Testament information we draw the conclusion that God wants families to follow Him together. Who can reach us better than our own flesh and blood? What bond is greater than the natural bond of siblings and parents?

Indeed, the fellowship these disciples enjoyed and the unity among them is easy to understand when you realize they had grown up together. To think that in their secluded region of Galilee, the Messiah would come and walk among them!

Matthew was a little different from the other disciples. His occupation tells us much about him. He was a publican. This meant he was a tax collector for the hated Roman Government. While the other disciples fished or farmed or worked in various trades of respect and industry, Matthew's profession was despised deeply among the people.

Publicans were always classed with sinners in the speech of the day. A common complaint against Jesus was "Why eateth your Master with publicans and sinners?" (Matthew 9:11). Rome's iron grip on Judea intensified this natural animosity toward the publicans.

One of Jesus' disciples, Simon Zelotes — who was a rumored brother of Matthew, James and Thaddeus — was a member of a fanatic political sect that sought the complete overthrow of the Roman yoke on Judea. As a publican, therefore, Matthew was despised by the highly nationalistic Jews.

His occupation tells us another thing about Matthew. His work necessitated keen intelligence. A tax collector had to be a keeper of records and detail. He had to be acquainted with the families and occupations of his community.

He had developed a knowledge of the people, along with their habits and idiosyncrasies. Since he was despised, he probably had to give a lot of thought as to how to cope and live successfully in spite of the handicap created by his work. Without a doubt, Matthew was a clever and resourceful person.

All of these qualities would serve him well as a disciple and writer of the first Gospel. One of the beautiful things about God is His ability to take us and use the qualities in our life for His glory.

God used Jonah's ability to convince his listeners; for at the preaching of Jonah, the people of Nineveh repented.

God saw David courageously defending his sheep from a marauding lion and a hungry bear. So when a champion was needed to fight Goliath, David was the logical choice.

Lydia, a woman of Thyratira who lived in Phillipi of Macedonia, was a seller of purple and a lady of prominence. When she was converted and baptized, God used her wealth and influence to sustain and protect Paul and Silas on their missionary journey.

God doesn't always give us new talents, although He certainly has both the ability and prerogative. But He does take what we have and He uses it. He needs only Moses' staff, Samson's jawbone, Shamgar's oxgoad, David's sling or the little lad's lunch to accomplish His greatest purposes.

God took a tax collector of Judea with an eye for detail and an ability to gather facts and used him to write the story of Jesus in order to win a lost world.

THE LINEAGE OF CHRIST

Matthew's Gospel is filled with wonder and awe as the story of Jesus unfolds. In the early verses we are given the fleshly lineage of Christ; yet, even in that lineage (which some find to be monotonous reading) we see God's love revealed to Adam's fallen race.

The first verse of Matthew's Gospel identifies Jesus as "The son of David, the son of Abraham." His kingship is immediately established as the son of David, Israel's greatest king. Jesus is King over all of Abraham's seed. He is King of the faithful.

The second verse of Matthew shows the covenant lineage going through Isaac and Jacob, not Ishmael or Esau. He comes from Jacob's son, Judah, who is the father of the royal line of Judah. Jacob had prophesied, "The sceptre shall not depart from Judah, nor a lawgiver from between his feet, until Shiloh come; and unto him shall the gathering of the people be" (Genesis 49:10).

As Matthew continues this lineage he notes Christ relationship with all people:

✓ Thamar and Rahab are unclean people in Christ's lineage, indicating that Christ is indeed the sinners' Friend.

✓ Rahab a Canaanite, and Ruth a Moabitess are ancestors of Jesus. Gentile blood mingles with the Hebrew blood, for Christ has come to break down the wall of partition and bless all the nations of the earth.

✓ Rahab was a harlot, and Jesus relates to fallen humanity.

✓ Ruth was a rustic woman from the hard country, and Jesus loves the lowly.

✓ Christ, as a descendant of Solomon in Matthew 5:6, teaches us that God forgave the sin of David and Bathsheba and blessed their seed in Solomon. This indicates the profound ability of God to forgive the vilest sin.

In the lineage of Christ are wayward kings and captive prisoners. There are obscure people and those of little note who hardly make a mark on the pages of history. But what insight Matthew gives us!

This lineage teaches us that God in the flesh contained the blood of people and represents the diversity of humanity! Christ died for all; none are excluded from His atoning and redemptive power.

He grew up in the house of a carpenter from Nazareth. He is the poor man's King and the Lord of the loveless and the leper. God will condescend to men of the lowest estate. Can we fathom such love? Can we ever express enough gratitude to God for the depths of such heavenly care?

Matthew, a detailed expositor of truth, has now given us the backdrop for Jesus' life. He is to be a Messiah of all with the exclusion of none. There can be no doubt that Matthew was deeply devoted to the principle of his people accepting Christ as the Messiah.

FULFILLMENT OF PROPHECY

Throughout this first Gospel, Matthew takes the various incidents in the life of Christ and shows how each one fulfilled a prophecy of the Old Testament.

In Matthew 1:18-21, he tells of Christ's virgin birth through Mary. He begins verse 22 by saying,

> Now all this was done, that it might be fulfilled which was spoken of the Lord by the prophet, saying, Behold, a virgin shall be with

child, and shall bring forth a son, and they shall call his name Emmanuel, which being interpreted is, God with us" (vv. 22, 23).

Matthew quoted from Isaiah 7:14, the prophet's famous Messianic prophecy to King Ahaz.

When he recorded the place of Christ's birth, Bethlehem, he quoted Micah 5:2, which states that the Messiah would be born in Bethlehem. Again he used the phrase, "For thus it is written by the prophet" (Matthew 2:5), to remind his Jewish readers that the Old Testament was being fulfilled in Christ.

When Herod attempted to destroy Jesus as an infant by slaughtering the innocent babies of Bethlehem, Matthew reminded his readers of the prophecy in Jeremiah 31:15, where weeping for the slain children was prophesied. He said that:

✓ Hosea predicted Christ would go to Egypt (Hosea 11:1; Matthew 2:15);

✓ John the Baptist was the fulfillment of Isaiah's prophecy (Isaiah 40:3; Matthew 3:3);

✓ Isaiah said Messiah would minister to Zabulon and Nephthalim (Isaiah 9:1-2; Matthew 4:13-16);

✓ the prophet had said Christ would heal the sick (Isaiah 53:4; Matthew 8:16-17);

✓ Christ would reach out to the Gentiles (Isaiah 42:1-4; Matthew 12:16-21);

✓ the prophet Jonah's ordeal was a sign of the resurrection (Jonah 1:17; Matthew 12:39-40); and

✓ Zechariah prophesied that the Messiah would enter Jerusalem on an ass's colt (Zechariah 9:9; Matthew 21:1-5).

In Matthew 24:15, Christ himself quotes the prophet Daniel (Daniel 9:27; 11:31; 12:11) as a stern warning concerning the great tribulation period. When Judas died and his burial place was purchased with his ill-gotten 30 pieces of silver, Matthew tells the reader that this was a fulfillment of prophecy (Matthew 27:9-10; Zechariah 11:12, 13).

When Christ died on Calvary and His executioners gambled for His parted garments, Matthew quoted the psalmist, "They parted my garments among them and upon my vesture did they cast lots" (Matthew 27:35; Psalm 22:18).

Matthew's message is clear and simple. Jesus of Nazareth is the fulfillment of Old Testament Messianic scriptures. He is the Christ; of that there can be no doubt.

Matthew's account of the Sermon on the Mount gives us some of Jesus' clearest teachings. From these beautiful words we learn about our daily walk with God. Chapters 5 through 7 record the discourse to the assembled people on the mountain. Here we find the Beatitudes, which tell us how to be blessed of the Lord (Matthew 5:1-12). These timeless pearls of divine wisdom prove themselves true every time they come alive and are active in a human heart.

The beatitudes tell of the rewards of meekness, humility, compassion, spiritual thirst, mercy, holiness, and peacemaking. A careful examination of these godly traits show they must come from a pure heart.

Christ then methodically deals with "traditions of men" versus the true will of the Heavenly Father. Their traditions dealt with murder, but Jesus taught that in the eyes of God, disdain and hatred of a neighbor was equally reprehensible (Matthew 5:21, 22).

He taught that the blessings of God never come to an unforgiving heart (vv. 23, 24), and that a heart full of carnal lust is as evil as the act of adultery itself (vv. 27, 28). He taught the horrors of hell (vv. 29, 30); the sanctity of marriage vows (vv. 31, 32); the care of our words (vv. 33-37); and the need to love and care for even our enemies (vv. 39-48).

Religious hypocrisy came under Christ's direct rebuke. He didn't stop with the condemnation of improper behavior, however; He took time to impart the proper way to do things.

For instance, He condemned their tendency to pray aloud, to "be seen of men" (Matthew 6:5); then

He told them how to pray in secret in order to be rewarded openly (v. 6). He spoke of forgiveness, fasting, heavenly treasures and the worthlessness of worry (vv. 14-34).

The Sermon on the Mount was a sermon for mankind from the Son of God Himself. To live this sermon is to please God and to obtain divine favor. Matthew was prompted by the Holy Spirit, through divine inspiration, to record this marvelous message.

From his account of this sermon, we learn more about Matthew's character. He is deeply touched by the words of Christ. He records miracles, healings and stories of Christ's power to deliver, but the words of Jesus are paramount in Matthew's mind. They are the key to eternal life (John 6:68).

The 24th and 25th chapters are paramount in our understanding of last-day eschatology, and they are almost entirely the recorded words of Jesus. How bankrupt Christianity would be without God's servant Matthew, the detail man, giving us these words of everlasting life.

THE GREAT COMMISSION

Finally, Matthew records the most powerful commission found in scripture. So powerful are these words that they have endured the scrutiny of time and have retained the title, "The Great Commission."

To examine them and try to dissect them is pointless, for they are plain words with a plain message from the resurrected Son of God.

It is an honor and a privilege to read them, to write them or to quote these words and let them speak as they have spoken to the ages:

> Go ye therefore, and teach all nations, baptizing them in the name of the Father, and of the Son and of the Holy Ghost: Teaching them to observe all things whatsoever I have commanded you: and lo, I am with you always, even unto the end of the world. Amen (Matthew 28:19, 20).

Thank you, Jesus! Thank you, Matthew.

> *My Jesus, I love Thee,*
> *I know Thou art mine;*
> *For thee all the follies*
> *Of sin I resign;*
> *My gracious Redeemer,*
> *My Savior Art Thou;*
> *If ever I loved Thee;*
> *My Jesus, 'tis now.*
>
> – A. J. Gordon

Matthew, the King Announcer

And as Jesus passed forth from thence, he saw a man named Matthew, sitting at the receipt of custom: and he saith unto him, Follow me. And he arose, and followed him (Matthew 9:9).

INTRODUCTION

Matthew's Gospel is a very special book in the Bible. For the first two centuries after Christ, it was the Gospel most frequently quoted by the early church fathers. First of four profound portraits of Jesus, Matthew goes into intricate detail to link the Old and New Testaments.

Jesus is beautifully presented as Israel's Messiah and long-awaited King. Matthew gives us a Jesus who is King, Servant and Son of the Living God.

I. MATTHEW'S FOUR PORTRAITS OF CHRIST

A. A biographical portrait of Christ

   1. Each event is a fulfillment of Old Testament messianic prophecy.

   2. Each event in Christ's life has a divine purpose.

B. A theological portrait of Christ

   1. He wrote to answer Jewish questions.

    2. He wrote to prepare Jewish converts to defend Christ's messiahship.

  C. An ethical portrait of Christ

    1. The Sermon on the Mount (*Matthew 5-7*)

    2. Heart motivations — basis for His judgment

      a. Lust is the same as adultery (*Matthew 5:27, 28*).

      b. Hate is the same as murder (*Matthew 5:21, 22*).

  D. An evangelistic portrait of Christ

    1. Last-day judgements foretold (*Matthew 24-25*)

    2. The Great Commission (*Matthew 28:19*)

II. GLIMPSE OF MATTHEW THE DISCIPLE

  A. He had three brothers who were disciples (James, Thaddeus, Simon Zelotes).

  B. He was a hated tax collector (*Matthew 9:9*).

    1. This means he was a "detail person."

    2. This would serve him well as a Gospel writer.

  C. Upon conversion, he invited Jesus to his home to talk to other sinners (*Matthew 9:11*).

  D. He was keenly intelligent, because the Romans recruited the most skillful and intelligent. God recruits talent for His kingdom.

  E. Matthew followed Jesus immediately without hesitation (*Matthew 9:9*).

Outline

III. MATTHEW'S USE OF CHRIST'S LINEAGE

A. Matthew 1:1 — As the Son of David, Jesus is identified as being from the tribe of Judah, a rightful heir to the throne and a Kinsman of David. As Son of Abraham, He is the spiritual heir to Israel's leadership.

B. Matthew 1:2 — Christ came from Jacob, not Esau; therefore He is a child of the covenant.

C. His lineage with Thamar, Rahab, Ruth, Bathsheba and Solomon identifies him with sinners and with the meek and lowly. Christ is the sinners' friend.

IV. MATTHEW BELIEVED THAT THE PROPHETS FORETOLD THE COMING OF JESUS.

A. He used prophetic scriptures throughout his book (*chapters 1, 3, 4, 8, 12, 21, 24, 27*).

B. He taught that Christ came not to destroy the law, but to fulfill it.

V. MATTHEW TAUGHT THAT CHRIST IS THE LORD OF OUR DAILY LIVES

A. He included the Sermon on the Mount as a guide for everyday living (*Matthew 5-7*).

B. He emphasized Christ's hatred of religious hypocrisy (*Matthew 6:5*).

C. He detailed Christ's last-days warnings (*Matthew 24, 25*).

Outline

VI. MATTHEW RECORDS THE GREAT COMMISSION.

A. The Great Commission tells us that the gospel is for the whole world.

B. The Great Commission is a mandate of action (*Matthew 28:19, 20*).

   1. Go

   2. Teach

   3. Baptize

   4. Observe all things I have commanded you

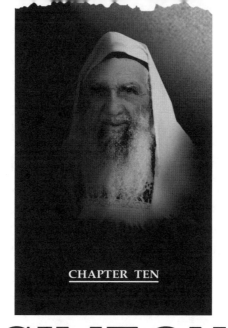

CHAPTER TEN

SIMEON AND ANNA
Persistent Prophets

And, behold, there was a man in Jerusalem, whose name was Simeon; and the same man was just and devout, waiting for the consolation of Israel: and the Holy Ghost was upon him . . . And there was one Anna, a prophetess, . . . which departed not from the temple, but served God with fastings and prayers night and day (Luke 2:25, 36, 37).

EVER SO OFTEN, IF ONE STUDIES SCRIPTURE LONG ENOUGH, he or she will come upon characters who are only mentioned briefly, but their one appearance in the pages of Holy Writ is so profound and their actions are of such impact, they are forever embedded in our memory.

The widow who fed Elijah, Nathan and his message to David, the woman who touched the hem of Jesus' garment, and the little lad who brought his loaves and fishes to the Master are almost anonymous people, but we shall never forget them.

Likewise, we can never think of the birth and infancy of Jesus without remembering Anna and Simeon.

A FAITHFUL REMNANT

So little is written of Christ's childhood that we cling to every word, lest some golden nugget of information escape our store of knowledge. At this time in Christ's infancy we see these ancient Hebrew saints, and through them, the faithful remnant in Israel who were looking for the Messiah.

This faithful remnant not only existed during this most difficult time, but if Anna and Simeon are to be understood as typical examples of the remnant, then these people were the spiritual giants of their day. In the worst of times and in the most difficult places, God has people who are faithful to Him.

The entire world was corrupt in the days just prior to the flood, "But Noah found grace in the sight of the Lord" (Genesis 6:8).

Elijah thought that Israel was so entrenched in idolatry under Ahab and Jezebel, that he alone was serving God; but the Lord reminded him that, "Yet I have left me seven thousand in Israel, all the knees which have not bowed unto Baal" (1 Kings 19:18).

God's true people remain faithful to Him in spite of adverse circumstances and the abundance of sin around them. No wonder Paul stated to the Roman church, which served God in one of the most wicked cities in history, "Where sin abounded, grace did much more abound" (Romans 5:20).

An evil, unsettled atmosphere pervaded in the days of Christ's birth. Rome, that iron beast of nations, ruled the known world. The Empire's foot pressed hard upon the neck of Judea in particular, because of constant uprisings. The people were taxed into poverty; survival was a task for all.

AN OPPRESSED PEOPLE

Glory days of Israel under David and Solomon were but ancient stories recited to children and passed from one generation to the next.

Zealots and Jewish nationalists tried to stir up insurrection; but more often than not, they wound up as crucified martyrs to a hopeless cause. The Roman eagle soared higher and higher, and the tramping of the boots of Caesar's legions gave despair a new sound. No doubt some resigned themselves to the life of a conquered and defeated people. Others thought of rebellion.

But there was a remnant who looked for Messiah. Desperately, these people believed the day would come when God would send a deliverer, just as He had sent one to their forefathers in Egypt.

Perhaps many thought this deliverer would come as a Joshua or a David, with awesome military skill coupled with divine power, and would shatter Rome's heavy yoke.

But the truly spiritual remnant realized Israel's plight was a matter of hearts out of tune with God. They knew that a prophet and a priest with the Word of God upon His lips was Israel's only hope.

Among this remnant we find two ancient seers named Anna and Simeon. Both were old and in the declining years of their lives. The spring of youth is long gone from their step, but their hearts burned with eternal fire. Both of these saints were led by the Spirit.

Since he is mentioned first, let us look first at Simeon. The name *Simeon* means "hearing," and even a cursory glance at this man reveals him to be a listener. His ears were keen and his spirit was watchful. He dwelt in Jerusalem and evidently stayed close to the Temple.

SIMEON, LISTENING PROPHET

Luke says that Simeon was "just and devout" (2:25) — terms that describe a man honest in his dealings with both God and man. Righteousness was a way of life for Simeon, and therefore it is no surprise that Luke's next comment was, "The Holy Ghost was upon him."

The Spirit of the Lord chooses only clean and worthy temples in which to dwell (see 1 Corinthians 6:19). Simeon was an earthly temple worthy of God's Spirit, and this relationship enabled him to listen to God's Spirit within Him.

The Spirit had given Simeon a life-guiding message of hope. Luke uses the Greek word *chrematidzo* to describe the communication imparted to Simeon by the Holy Ghost. It means "to admonish, warn and reveal."

The Holy Spirit had admonished Simeon that he would not die until he had seen "the Lord's Christ" (Luke 2:26). Therefore, his whole life was subservient to this prophecy, as he waited for "the consolation of Israel" (Luke 2:25). Here is a saint of the old covenant waiting for the Maker of the new covenant.

He stayed near the Temple, for he was aware of the Mosaic Law regarding the circumcision of newborn males in Israel. Baby boys were brought to the temple for consecration and circumcision, and an offering of a lamb, two turtledoves or a pair of pigeons would be given to God (see Numbers 18:15).

A MISSION FULFILLED

On the 8th day of Jesus' life, He was brought to the Temple by Mary and Joseph for circumcision, to comply with Leviticus 12:3. The Bible says that on that same day Simeon "came by the Spirit into the temple" (Luke 2:27).

Here we see a man who not only listens to God's Spirit, but who is obedient to the leading of the Spirit. "For many be called, but few chosen" (Matthew 20:16). Only a listener who obeys will receive the benefits of God's calling.

Because Simeon was an active listener who obeyed divine direction, God's blessed Spirit had brought him to the moment he had spent most of his life waiting for. One wonders what must have gone through Simeon's mind when he saw Jesus.

The wonder and rapture he felt must have thrilled and fulfilled him. The Messiah had come!

Even if no one else in the Temple was aware of it that day, this elderly and devout prophet knew that the little Boy he was about to hold was the Redeemer of the world.Simeon took baby Jesus in his arms and held Him.

Though Isaiah had prophesied that the Child would come (see Isaiah 9:6), that great statesman-prophet of Israel was not here to behold Him.

Though Micah had pinpointed Bethlehem as His birthplace (Micah 5:2), the fiery prophet would never cradle the Baby in his arms.

Although Hosea told of His flight to Egypt (see Hosea 11:1) and Jeremiah spoke of Herod's treachery to kill Him (see Jeremiah 31:15), neither of these great seers would hold the little Baby in their arms.

God entrusted his faithful servant, Simeon, with this warm and wonderful task. As Simeon took the Child in his arms, he praised God. Such a moment is designed for praise. God had now sent His Son into the world. Salvation from the curse of Eden's garden was now provided.

One wants to worship with Simeon and cry with the caroling angels, "Glory to God in the highest" (Luke 2:14). And raise a powerful anthem of praise with the seraphim, "Holy, holy, holy, is the Lord of Host: the whole earth is full of his glory!" (Isaiah 6:3).

Simeon's praise continues with this prayer, "Lord, now lettest thou thy servant depart in peace" (Luke 2:29). Literally translated this reads, "Now thou art setting free Thy bond-slave, Despot." The word "despot" is offensive to some because of its evil connotations.

But this is the word Simeon used. He is saying, "I am a bond-slave under authority held by the dictates of the Law; but now, due to the arrival of the Redeemer, my death will not be dissolution but emancipation. I am set free!"

Simeon knew that the power of death would be broken forever by the appearance and deeds of this Child and his rejoicing at the tiny bundle in his arms was understandable. Then he declares, "Mine eyes have seen thy salvation" (Luke 2:30).

Simeon was the first to announce that Christ would not only lighten the glory of God's people Israel, but that he would be a "light to the Gentiles" (Luke 2:32). At that time the Gentile world was searching and groping in the darkness of misguided philosophy and barbarism.

Militaristic nations such as Rome were possessed with a conqueror's mindset. Like the Greeks and others, idolatry and fleshly immorality were so intermingled that many of these nations were akin to Sodom and Gomorrah; the knowledge of the true God was unknown to them. But now, the Babe in old Simeon's arms was a beacon of hope and salvation to these pitiful and misguided people.

At these words of Simeon, Mary and Joseph marveled, even though miraculous things had filled their life from the moment of Christ's conception.

It is as though a never-ending chain of supernatural events was continually reminding them of God's covering over all of these things.

Two more prophecies came from Simeon's lips. Both were given directly to Mary, Jesus' mother. She is told, "Behold, this child is set for the fall and rising again of many in Israel; and for a sign which shall be spoken against" (Luke 2:34).

Simeon is simply stating that for some in Israel, Jesus would be a stumbling stone of offense because they would reject Him and in so doing, reject eternal life and hope. Others would rise and call Him blessed and in so doing would secure for themselves and their loved ones the eternal redemption of God.

The word Simeon uses for "sign" is the Greek word *semeion*, meaning "a token or sign for divine confirmation." Christ's miracles and signs would have detractors and doubters; some would seek to discredit Him. His life would never be one of ease, and Simeon's prophecy prepared Mary for this.

His next words to her are even more poignant. "Yea, a sword shall pierce through your own soul also" (Luke 2:35). The word here is the Greek word *rhomphaia,* which means "extreme anguish." Only a mother could feel the kind of anguish Mary would feel at the sufferings of her son. It is as if as sword would be run through her soul, shattering her heart.

Simeon's prophecies came to pass precisely as he had spoken, and he leaves us with no doubt about his authenticity as a prophet of God.

ANNA, MESSIANIC MESSENGER

At this moment we are introduced to Anna. She was a prophetess of great age who represented women in the advent of the Messiah. Along with Elisabeth and Mary, she was one of those godly women that the Lord sent into the life of the infant Christ to show care and love to the Son of God.

According to the scripture, she had been a widow for 84 years and now lived in the Temple itself. There, the Bible says, she "served God with fastings and prayer night and day" (v. 37).

What a testimony of devotion! Here is a distinguished and noble lady of faith who longed for the courts of the Lord. Her life was under the control of the Spirit and she, like Simeon, served like a true servant. God heard her intercession and that of the remnant in Israel like her, and He sent the Redeemer.

She enters the scene with Joseph and Mary as Simeon was holding the Babe. From the moment of her entrance, she started giving thanks to God. She never ceased. Her gratitude erupted from her heart, and it was spontaneous.

Anna lifted her voice in prophecy, and this ancient widow declared to all who looked for redemption that this baby Boy was their answer. She made a messianic announcement.

John the Baptist would do likewise along a muddy river bank many years later when he cried, "Behold the Lamb of God, which taketh away the sin of the world" (John 1:29). Now the voice of these prophets is lifted up to proclaim the infant Jesus as Lord and Giver of life.

EXAMPLES OF HOPE

Anna and Simeon give us a marvelous glimpse of God's grace to people of all ages. Though elderly in body and weak in the flesh, their spirits remained strong, and they represented the human race's longing for salvation and hope.

They are examples to follow, and their righteousness speaks to all generations. The Baby they held that day would grow up and die on a cross, rise again the third day, and finally ascend to heaven 40 days later.

Today He is alive forevermore. He ever lives to make "intercession for the saints according to the will of God" (Romans 8:27).

Anna and Simeon knew of whom they spake.

A charge to keep I have,
A God to glorify;
Who gave his son my soul to save,
And fit it for the sky.

To serve the present age,
My calling to fulfill,
O may it all my pow'rs engage
To do my Master's will.

Arm me with jealous care,
As in Thy sight to live;
And O, Thy servant, Lord, prepare
A strict account to give!

-Charles Wesley

Anna and Simeon, Persistent Prophets

And, behold, there was a man in Jerusalem, whose name was Simeon; and the same man was just and devout, waiting for the consolation of Israel: and the Holy Ghost was upon him. And there was one Anna, a prophetess . . . which departed not from the temple, but served God with fastings and prayers night and day (Luke 2:25, 36, 37).

INTRODUCTION

One who studies the scriptures long enough will come upon characters who are mentioned only briefly, but their one appearance in the pages of Holy Writ is so profound and their actions of such impact that they are forever embedded in our memories.

The widow who fed Elijah, Nathan and his message to David, the woman who touched the hem of Jesus' garment and the little lad who brought his loaves and fishes to the Master are people, often unnamed, whom we shall never forget.

And we can never think of the birth and infancy of Jesus without remembering Anna and Simeon.

Outline

I. A FAITHFUL REMNANT IN ISRAEL LOOKED FOR THE MESSIAH.

A. *Luke 1 and 2* tell of Zacharias and Elizabeth, Mary and Joseph, the shepherds, and Anna and Simeon — all faithful people who looked for the Messiah.

B. Faithful people also look for His Second Coming. "Unto them that look for him shall he appear the second time without sin unto salvation" (*Hebrews 9:28*).

II. CHRIST CAME TO AN OPPRESSED PEOPLE.

A. Israel was under bondage to Rome.

B. The people were under bondage to religious legalism and traditions.

C. The human race was under bondage to sin.

III. SIMEON, THE LISTENING PROPHET

A. The name *Simeon* means "hearing".

B. Simeon was blessed with spiritual graces.

1. Just and devout (*Luke 2:25*)

2. Holy Ghost-anointed (*Luke 2:25*)

3. Promised that he would see Messiah before he died (*Luke 2:26*)

4. Patient (*Luke 2:25*)

Outline

IV. SIMEON'S MISSION WAS FULFILLED.

A. Simeon was led by the Spirit into the temple on the day of Christ's circumcision (*Luke 2:27*).

B. Simeon gave praise to God for sending Christ.
1. Angels praised God at His birth (*Luke 2:13-14*).
2. Angels praise Him in heaven now (*Revelation 5:13*).

C. Simeon fulfilled his mission as prophet.
1. Declared Christ to be the Savior (*Luke 2:30*)
2. Prophesied salvation to the Gentiles (*Luke 2:32*)
3. Foretold of Mary's sorrow at His death (*Luke 2:34-35*)

V. ANNA WAS A MESSIANIC ANNOUNCER.

A. She was a holy woman.

B. She served God through fasting and prayer (*Luke 2:37*).

C. She spoke to the temple crowd and proclaimed the baby Jesus to be the source of redemption (*Luke 2:38*).

VI. ANNA AND SIMEON EXEMPLIFIED HOPE.

A. Their hope of a Messiah became a reality.

B. Paul called the return of Christ, "that blessed hope" (*Titus 2:13*).

C. With hope, we have nothing to be ashamed of (*Romans 5:5*).

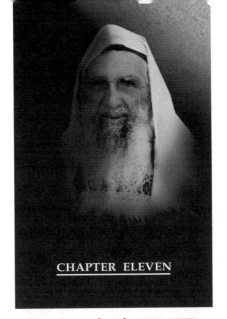

CHAPTER ELEVEN

PETER
Our Disciple

And Simon Peter answered and said, Thou art the Christ, the Son of the living God (Matthew 16:16).

AMONG THE 12 DISCIPLES OF JESUS, NONE WAS MORE VOCAL than the fisherman called Peter. And it is precisely his willingness to speak that causes most of us to identify with him.

We refer to him as "our disciple," because in his spoken words we see the best and the worst of humanity. He is the consummate human being. He is both weak and strong. He is both vengeful and merciful. He is both proud and humble. Peter is us. We see ourselves in every facet of his life, and it is a source of great comfort that Jesus loved Peter dearly, in spite of the complexity of his personality.

PETER'S CALLING

Peter is first seen along the coast of Galilee with his brother, Andrew. They are casting their net into the sea, " for they were fishers" (Matthew 4:18). Jesus was walking by the sea on this occasion and He said to them, "Follow me, and I will make you fishers of men" (Mathew 4:19).

Their response tells us much about these sons of Jonas. The Bible says, "They straightway left their nets, and followed him" (v. 20).

Their nets represented their livelihood. They had been raised to catch fish. Fishing was their life and provision. The Bible indicates that Peter himself was a married man, possibly with a family (see 8:14). Their bread and daily sustenance depended on their success in casting their nets, but they dropped those nets instantly at the beckoning of Lord Jesus.

Two things stand out in this calling. The first is obvious: there was power in the voice of Jesus. This power was compelling. No one who once hears His voice remains the same. Peter and Andrew were impressed by this voice. It wooed them from their menial and mundane daily tasks, and drew their hearts to a higher plane.

Secondly, we see the decisiveness of Peter and Andrew. There was no hesitation. They were attuned to the needs of their own spirits. The longing of their hearts suddenly became more important than the demands of the physical.

To "catch men" was an intriguing possibility. There was but one thing to do. The answer was simple — they followed him.

Galilee was the frontier of Judea. When the Promise Land was divided under Joshua, the area around Galilee was inhabited largely by the tribes of Naphtali, Manasseh and Zebulan. During the centuries of foreign rule and the upheaval of the Jewish people, there had been displacement and moving.

Galilee, however, basically remained a land of small villages, and the occupations practiced by the people were those things necessary to sustain rural life. The sea itself was a source of life. The water was cool and fresh, and there was an abundance of fish to be found in its depths. The coastal towns of Bethsaida, Capernaum, Magdala and Tiberias provided ports for fishermen who harvested the waters of the Galilee Sea.

The dialect and accent of the language spoken in

Galilee readily identified them to others in the Middle Eastern world. Galileans were considered backward, rural and were often held in contempt by the more sophisticated people of Jerusalem.

From this background of small farms, groves, tiny hamlets and fisherman's huts Christ grew to adulthood. From this same environment He chose men to follow Him. These disciples, from simple, rural Galilee, would shake the world and forever change the course of humanity by preaching the gospel of the Son of God.

God's method has always defied the logic of the so-called "wise" men of this earth. He chooses the foolish things to confound the wise. He prefers the weak to be used to overcome the strong.

No flesh can glory in His presence, because God does things in such a way—through seemingly unusable vessels—that there is no doubt that He, and He alone, is the source of the miracle.

PETER'S IMPERFECTIONS

Peter, the fisherman, was just such a vessel. Loud, brash, impetuous and quick of temper, he spoke with the slang and accent of Galilee and would probably be the average pulpit committee's last choice as a candidate to lead the infant body of Christ into a program of world evangelism. But

God chose him on the Day of Pentecost.

To understand this giant of the faith, it is important to look at him through an uncompromising lens of scrutiny. His faults must be seen as well as his triumphs.

The final picture of Simon Peter is never complete until you view his early days of learning. Here you see just what kind of granite block God chiseled him from. Flaws and imperfections had to be carefully removed until the divine artist crafted a masterpiece of honor, well equipped for the Lord's work.

PETER'S GROWTH

The first thing we notice in Peter's growth as a disciple was the fact that he, like all of the other disciples, had to learn to follow before he could ever become a leader.

His first step was to follow Christ when He called, but the journey is farther than the first step. His life's journey with Christ was filled with growth and discovery, not only about himself, but about the true nature of the kingdom of God.

In these steps of growth, we readily identify with the Big Fisherman. One dark night, in deep Galilee waters, the disciples were endeavoring to row their boat to the shore, and the elements of wave and water were working against them. That night Jesus came walking to them on the surface of the water. Now this miracle occurred between 3:00 a.m. and 6:00 a.m. on a dark and stormy night.

Earlier Jesus had "constrained" the disciples to get into a ship "to go before Him unto the other side" (Matthew 14:22), while He went to a mountain to pray (v. 23).

Note carefully that Jesus never sends us on a journey with an expressed destination unless He means for us to reach that destination. He had sent them "to the other side," and although they faced obstacles during the journey, Christ meant for them to complete it.

Their natural fear was already aroused by the wind and waves; but when they saw Him walking on the water, they became intensely afraid and cried out, saying that it was a spirit (v. 26). Jesus responded by telling them, "Be of good cheer; it is I; be not afraid" (v. 27).

Peter was the first to respond to this assurance. His bold question meant that if it was answered in the affirmative, this will force him to make a step of faith. He says, "Lord if it be thou, bid me come unto thee on the water" (v. 28). Jesus simply said, "Come."

Peter immediately stepped out of the boat and

the scriptures testify, "he walked on the water, to go to Jesus" (v. 29). Proper directional movement required him to look at his goal, which was Jesus. As long as his eyes were on the Master, He walked on the water. But the Bible says, "He saw the wind boisterous, he was afraid" (v. 30).

The miracle under his feet depended on his focused view of Christ; but when the circumstances of life diverted that focus, fear set in and he began to sink. The Sea of Galilee was cold and deep, and certain death awaited him in the depths. But the faith that had moved him out of the boat gave him wisdom for the moment of danger.

When some are sinking, they sink until they are sunk. Not so with Peter. He cried out, "Lord, save me" (v. 30). His companions were on a ship. No doubt ropes and even flotation devices were available, but he did not cry for their help or rescue. He knew who to cry for, and the response of Jesus was immediate.

"Immediately Jesus stretched forth his hand, and caught him" (v. 31). Not only did Jesus rescue him, but He also taught him the growth lesson by asking as He was lifting him from the pool of death, "O thou of little faith, wherefore didst thou doubt?" (v. 31).

Faith got Peter out of the boat and enabled him to walk on the water, but doubt almost cost him his life. Faith upholds; doubt sinks. Faith is the stuff of miracles; doubt brings tragedy. Faith guides us to the Master; doubt engulfs us in a watery grave. Peter had learned a valuable lesson.

Verse 32 tells us they came back to the ship and this raises a question: Did Peter walk back to the ship with Christ, or did Jesus carry him? Either answer is cause for rejoicing.

If Peter's faith was restored and the sea once again was a floor to his feet, we see a continuation of a great miracle. If, however, Christ lifted Peter and carried him back, we see another great miracle, which reminds us of God's power to carry us through our most difficult moments.

However they arrived, when they got back to the ship, the wind ceased. The sea would have engulfed them, but it was under the subjection of Christ's feet. The wind would have overwhelmed them, but He is the Master of the wind.

Another growth step in the life of Peter occurred at the transfiguration of Jesus. Peter, along with James and John, the sons of Zebedee, comprised what became known as Christ's inner circle. Matthew, Mark and Luke all record this event known as the Transfiguration of Christ.

Jesus took Peter, James and John with him into a high mountain. The Bible says he was "transfigured," a word from the original Greek *metamorphoo* which means "to change form." His face was as "bright as the sun" (Matthew 17:2) and his raiment was shining "white as snow; so as no fuller on earth can white them" (Mark 9:3). Moses and Elijah appeared, talking with Him.

Much speculation has been made about the meaning of this, but it would seem that Jesus is portrayed as the fulfillment of the law and the prophets. The law is represented by Moses and the prophets by Elijah. Also, Moses could represent the dead saints, and Elijah the raptured ones.

According to Luke, they also talked with Him about His death that would occur in Jerusalem (Luke 9:31). We do know that the disciples were heavy with sleep and awoke to see Christ and the two Patriarchs (Luke 9:32).

All three of the Synoptic Gospels record Simon Peter's speech. He began with an expression of rapturous feelings. Then he asked Jesus to build three tabernacles or shrines: one for Christ, one for Moses and one for Elijah (Matthew 17:4; Mark 9:5; Luke 9:33). This was Peter's exuberance coming out, but the request was exactly what God did not want. The Jews were too hung up on shrines, temples and monuments; Christ was the Savior of the living.

Also, it is important to understand that Moses

and Elijah vanished and only Jesus remained, indicating that He alone was to be worshiped. Moses and Elijah were men, not gods. All three writers record that God spoke and identified Jesus as His Son and commanded the disciples to "hear ye him" (Matthew 17:15; Mark 9:7; Luke 9:35).

God was saying, "Peter quit talking and making plans. Listen to My Son." It was a striking lesson that Peter would remember all of his life. Years later He wrote in his second epistle that he was one of the "eyewitnesses of [Jesus'] majesty" (2 Peter 1:16). He told of God's voice that he heard, and used the phrase, "when we were with him in the holy mount" (v. 18). Hearing God's voice made an indelible mark on Peter's heart.

Peter declared his belief that Jesus was the "Christ, the Son of the living God" at Caesarea Phillipi. Christ called him "blessed," saying the revelation came not from himself but from the heavenly Father (Matthew 16:16-18).

Jesus called him Peter from the Greek *Petros* and Aramaic *Keophas*. The name means a "fragment of rock" or "pebble."

Then Jesus teaches us the importance of words for He uses another word for *rock* when He says, "Upon this *rock* I will build my church." The word here is *Petra* which means an "immovable stone," like a gigantic boulder or mountain made of stone. Christ is saying, "Peter you are just a small stone, a man, a human being; but I will build my church on an immovable rock, namely the confession you just made that I am the Christ, the Son of the living God."

How ridiculous it is for anyone to think that the church is built on anyone less than Christ himself. Christ is the *Petra* stone, the Immovable Boulder. He is the Chief Cornerstone which the builders rejected.

Paul later said that the stone Moses struck in the wilderness was Christ (see 1 Corinthians 10:4). When David's heart was overwhelmed, he prayed for God to "Lead me to the rock that is higher than I. For thou hast been a shelter for me, and a strong tower from the enemy" (Psalm 61:2, 3).

Jesus is the rock of the church, not Peter. And Peter, of all people, knew that. In 1 Peter 2:7, 8 he called Christ "the stone . . . the same is made the head of the corner, And a stone of stumbling, and a rock of offence, even to them which stumble at the word, being disobedient: whereunto also they were appointed." Peter knew who the *Petra* stone was.

PETER'S DIFFICULTIES

Despite Peter's great confession of Christ's deity at Caesarea Philipi, he still had much to learn. Five verses later, he was rebuked by Christ.

In Matthew 16:21, Jesus began to outline His arrest, trial and death to the disciples. Peter called Him aside to rebuke this talk. Instead, Jesus sternly rebuked him. Peter's humanity was obvious again. The thought of Christ's death appalled him.

He did not want Jesus to wash his feet at the Last Supper, because He didn't understand fully Christ's lesson of servanthood (see John 13:8).

Peter took his sword and cut off the High Priest's servant's ear as he attempted to stop the arrest of Jesus (see 18:10). No doubt he sought to kill him. Jesus immediately healed the man, whose name was Malchus, and restored the severed ear (Luke 22:51).

The story of Peter's denial of Christ on the night of his trial has been told often through the centuries. Jesus prophesied it would happen in Luke 22:34, and indeed Peter denied Christ three times before the cock crowed announcing the dawn of the day of Jesus' death (see vv. 54-60).

When the shrill sound of the rooster's crow was heard, Peter went out and wept bitterly (v. 62). This was one of the most powerful moments in Peter's life. Remorse and repentance always affect us like this.

Tears are the river to the soul, and Peter's river

overran its banks on that bitter dawn. He had denied the One he loved so much. He had fallen prey to his own fears and pathetic humanity. The revelations of the Mount and the confession of Caesarea Philipi seemed so distant now. The Big Fisherman was a sobbing soul of regret and remorse.

PETER'S FORGIVENESS

One has to wonder if Peter would have ever forgiven himself had it not been for something an angel said. Self-forgiveness is often the most difficult forgiveness of all. After the resurrection of Christ, an angel clothed in a long white garment told the women standing before the empty tomb:

> Ye seek Jesus of Nazareth, which was crucified: he is risen; he is not here: behold the place where they laid him. But go your way and tell his disciples and Peter that he goeth before you into Galilee (Mark 16:6, 7).

Here we find God specifically telling the women that Jesus not only wants to see His disciples, but that He especially wants to see Peter. He loved Peter. He had already forgiven Peter.

Then, Jesus asked Peter by the seaside if he still loved Him. He asked this three times, and, with each asking, He commanded Peter to feed his sheep as a sign of that love (see John 21:15-17).

Jesus also told Peter that he would die as an old man against his own will, signifying that Peter would die a martyr's death (see vv. 17-19).

By now everything was all right. Peter addressed the multitude on the Day of Pentecost when the church exploded in growth with the outpouring of the Holy Spirit (Acts 2).

- ✓ Peter was with John when they prayed for the lame man at the gate called Beautiful in Acts 3.

- ✓ Peter was in the midst of the great Samaritan revival in Acts 8.

- ✓ Peter was the first to preach the gospel to the Gentiles and see the Holy Spirit poured out on them at the house of Cornelius in Acts 10.

Peter proves that common men, with all their faults, are still candidates to be vessels for God's glory. His life is a portrait of trial and error, mistake and triumph, failure and victory, and God's ultimate forgiveness and provision of anointing.

We should not lionize Peter. Nor should we disdain him. He was just a man.

But Christ died for men, and Peter himself later

died for the cause of Christ.

Like Peter, our hope is in the Rock, Christ Jesus!

My hope is built on nothing less
Than Jesus' blood and righteousness;
I dare not trust the sweetest frame,
but wholly lean on Jesus' name.

On Christ, the solid Rock, I stand;
All other ground is sinking sand,
All other ground is sinking sand.

– Edward Mote

Peter, Our Disciple

*Simon Peter answered and said, Thou art the Christ,
the Son of the living God* (Matthew 16:16).

INTRODUCTION

Among the 12 disciples of Jesus, none was more
vocal than the fisherman called Peter; it is precisely
his willingness to speak that causes most of us to
identify with him. We refer to him as "our
disciple," because in his spoken words we see the
best and the worst of humanity.

He is the consummate human being. He is both
weak and strong. He is vengeful and merciful. He is
proud and humble. Peter is us. We see ourselves in
every facet of his life, and it is a source of great
comfort that Jesus loved Peter dearly, in spite of the
variety of qualities in his personality.

I. THE CALLING OF PETER

A. To understand Peter, you must understand Galilee.

1. A rural, hard land

2. A land of hardworking people (fishermen,
   tradesmen, carpenters, and so forth)

Outline

    3. An unlikely place for God's Son to come from, but the perfect place from which to speak to humanity.

B. Peter and Andrew were called at the same time.

    1. They left immediately.

    2. He called them to be "fishers of men."

II. PETER, THE IMPERFECT VESSEL

A. There were flaws in his character.

B. Glimpses of greatness were often seen in him.

C. Christ allowed Peter to learn.

III. PETER'S STEPS OF GROWTH

A. The night he walked on the water (*Matthew 14:22-33*)

    1. A night of faith—he walked (*Matthew 14:29*)

    2. A night of failure—he sank (*Matthew 14:30*)

    3. A night of salvation—"Jesus stretched forth his hand, and caught him" (*Matthew 14:31*).

B. Christ's Transfiguration (*Luke 9, Matthew 17, Mark 9*)

    1. He went to the mountain with Jesus.

    2. He saw the glorious vision.

    3. He talked when he should have listened.

    4. He was rebuked by God himself.

  C. His great day at Caesarea Philipi (*Matthew 16*)

    1. He declared Jesus to be the Christ.

    2. Jesus "blessed him."

    3. He was informed that he was only a small stone (*Matthew 16:18*).

    4. He was told that Christ would build the church on the fact that He, Jesus, was the Son of God.

IV. PETER'S HARD LESSONS

  A. Rebuked for disputing Christ's mission of death (*Matthew 16:21-23*)

  B. Attempted the murder of Malchus, the High Priest's servant (*John 18:10; Luke 22:51*)

  C. Tried to deny Christ's right to wash his feet (*John 13:8*)

  D. Denied knowing Jesus (*Luke 22:54-62*)

V. PETER'S FORGIVENESS AND COMMISSION

  A. After the Resurrection, he was told to meet with Jesus (*Mark 16:6-7*).

  B. He was told, "If you love me, feed my sheep" (*John 21:15-17*).

  C. He preached the great Day of Pentecost sermon (*Acts 2*).

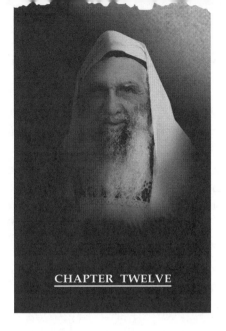

CHAPTER TWELVE

BARTIMAEUS
The Blind Witness

As he went out of Jericho with his disciples and a great number of people, blind Bartimaeus, the son of Timaeus, sat by the highway side begging. And when he heard that it was Jesus of Nazareth, he began to cry out, and say, Jesus, thou Son of David, have mercy on me (Mark 10:46, 47).

DEATH CAME STALKING HUMANITY WEARING THE CLOAK OF SICKNESS. Since the curse on Adam and Eve, sickness and disease have ravaged the human race. Sin has brought forth death. One of the reasons Jesus came was to heal. Isaiah prophesied of the complete mission of the Messiah, and Jesus quoted this prophecy of Himself in the synagogue at Nazareth:

The Spirit of the Lord is upon me, because he hath anointed me to preach the gospel to the poor; he hath sent me to heal the broken-hearted, to preach deliverance to the captives, and recovering of sight to the blind, to set at liberty them that are bruised, To preach the acceptable year of the Lord (Luke 4:18, 19; see also Isaiah 61:1, 2).

Jesus came to heal. This fact is evident in both His life and His sufferings leading to His death.

JERICHO, THE CITY

Jericho, known so well for its palm trees it is called "the city of palm trees," sits in the hot, dry landscape just north of the Dead Sea.

A primary route of travel runs through Jericho, and travelers used this route in their journeys from Galilee to Jerusalem. It was a sort of oasis in the desert; for centuries, caravans and pilgrims have stopped beneath the shade of its palms and have drunk from its cool wells.

To this day merchants hawk their wares here; innkeepers sell food and drink to weary sojourners.

The city was the site of one of Israel's greatest victories in the days of Joshua, when its walls "fell down flat" (Joshua 6:5) as the children of Israel marched and shouted praises to God (see vv.1-21). In this city Jesus demonstrated His healing power over blindness to four different blind men.

Luke tells of a blind man healed "as [Jesus] was come nigh to Jericho" (Luke 18:35-43). Matthew tells of two blind men healed as Jesus "departed from Jericho" (Matthew 20:29-34).

Mark tells the story of Bartimeus, the son of Timeus, who was healed as Jesus "went out" of Jericho (Mark 10:46-52).

Some speculate that these stories are one and the same, but each gospel writer tells of different circumstances and different locations for the healings.

Eye disease is common in the Middle East. The brightness of the sun, the lack of shade, the blowing sand — all contribute to the fact that eye disease and blindness affects one in five people in that part of the world.

In the days of Jesus, it was not uncommon, in a large city like Jericho, to find four blind men. And in those days, begging was their only means of sustenance; so compassionate friends would often take them to the busier thoroughfares of travel where more people could be found.

There blind men begged for food and money. Nor is it odd that Jesus would heal all four, for His mission was "that sight might be restored to the blind."

BARTIMAEUS, THE BLIND MAN

Mark, however, chose to personalize the story of one of these blind men. He gave the beggar a name. Mark identifies him and tells who his father is, and we feel closer to this blind man named Bartimaeus.

The man who was healed displayed remarkable character and faith; and although we only see him in these few verses, the virtues he demonstrates are examples for us all.

As Jesus left Jericho, Bartimaeus was at his usual spot doing as he had done most of his life — begging. That he was known as "blind Bartimaeus" (Mark 10:46) tells us he may have been this way most of his life.

It is said that when one of the five senses fail, the others become much more acute, especially the hearing. The survival of the blind man depended on his keen hearing, smell, taste and touch. Blind men have little to do but listen; but listening would be the salvation of Bartimaeus.

The Bible teaches that we are to train ourselves to listen more. God wants us to hear; and through hearing, understand. James said, "Wherefore, my beloved brethren, let every man be swift to hear, slow to speak, slow to wrath" (James 1:19).

Bartimaeus heard the sound of the approaching crowd that day as Jesus went out of Jericho.

Perhaps he was sitting in the shadow of the city gate or under a palm by the roadside as the huge entourage of people thronged the Master.

The keen ears of this astute blind man quickly perceived that it was Jesus of Nazareth. For months he had heard this name. He had listened to countless discussions and debates about whether Jesus was the Messiah.

At some point, Bartimaeus settled the issue in his mind. He knew who Jesus was. He believed Him to be the Messiah. That belief, coupled with a powerful desire for deliverance, prompted him to do what he did.

Mark says, "And when he heard that it was Jesus of Nazareth, he began to cry out, and say, Jesus, thou Son of David, have mercy on me" (Mark 10:47). It was the cry of a needy man! It was the cry of faith, verbalized and plain! It was the cry of a believer in the Messiah! He knew Jesus to be "the Son of David."

His eyes may have been blind, but his heart had perfect vision. After all, it is the vision of the heart that touches God. What a man knows in his heart often defies what his eyes tell him.

Paul said, "While we look not at the things which are seen, but at the things which are not seen: for the things which are seen are temporal; but the things which are not seen are eternal" (2 Corinthians 4:18). Bartimaeus knew who he cried to, though his natural eyesight was gone.

At his cry, the people around him began to reprimand and rebuke him. They demanded that this blind beggar be silent. How often do we let pomp and circumstance, protocol and decorum, affect the manifestation of our faith?

People with physical handicaps often suffer from certain attitudes that society as a whole exhibits toward them. They are often shoved out of sight and taken off the stage, lest we have to deal with their condition. Whatever their reasons, the crowd around him tried to silence blind Bartimaeus.

The true man or woman of faith does not have to acquiesce to the opinions of the majority. What does he or she have to lose? The need is greater and faith is more powerful than the needs of protocol.

JESUS, THE SUFFERER'S SAVIOR

The Bible is explicit in describing Bartimaeus' reaction to the crowd's rebuke. "He cried the more a great deal, Thou Son of David, have mercy on me" (Mark 10:48). The reaction of Jesus to Bartimaeus is a lesson for the ages. Scripture records, "And Jesus stood still" (10:49). The Master stopped. The urgency of this cry halted the parade. There would be no further travel until this situation was dealt with.

Jesus, like Bartimaeus, was also a listener.

- ✓ When Peter was sinking beneath the waves and cried, "Lord save me, Jesus listened.

- ✓ When Jairus said, "My little daughter lieth at the point of death, Jesus listened.

- ✓ When Andrew said, "There is a little lad here with five loaves and two fishes," Jesus listened. He hears us. His ears are never deafened to our cry and prayer. Bartimaeus cried and Jesus stood still.

But this story doesn't end with Jesus' listening ear. He reacted; Jesus summoned Bartimaeus. The people said unto him, "Be of good comfort, rise; he calleth thee" (v. 49). The relief that must have ensued was most wonderful. Can you imagine what surged through the blind man's heart at hearing these words? "I am going to Jesus," he must have thought.

This would be the last time Jesus would pass through Jericho. Blacksmiths say, "Strike while the iron is hot!" Bartimaeus knew in his spirit that his cry must be heard, for there would be no other time to make the cry.

And Jesus stood still.

The next thing Bartimaeus does demonstrates even more the remarkable character of this blind man. "And he, casting away his garment, rose, and came to Jesus" (v. 50).

Perhaps the garment was heavy and impeded his rapid movement. Perhaps it contained all of his possessions—his cup, his meager food and personal items. In any case, the garment represented his former life, and, in faith, he cast it aside. He would no longer need it.

When we go to Jesus, we must put the past behind us. The former life of sin and spiritual blindness encumbers and weighs one down. Casting it aside is a statement of faith. We are saying to the world, "We have found a new direction. Old things have been cast away and all things are now new" (see 2 Corinthians 5:17).

As sinners, we once begged for sustenance and were blind to the light of the truth. But when the Master beckons, the garments of our spiritual poverty are no longer needed. We walk in the light as He is in the light.

Jesus asked Bartimaeus what he wanted. This might seem strange to some, but prayer is an act of seeking, asking and knocking. To request is to express faith that the request will be granted. Bartimaeus was quick in his response, "Lord that I might receive my sight" (Mark 10:51). His intent now stated, he boldly made his request known to the only one who could grant it.

Oh, for the boldness of a request of faith. So often we don't have because we don't ask. We are afraid to ask for the impossible, because we fear disappointment.

But God is impressed with bold faith. "Let us therefore come boldly unto the throne of grace, that we may obtain mercy, and find grace to help in time of need" (Hebrews 4:16).

HEALING, THE TRIUMPH OF FAITH

Jesus was quick to reward such bold faith. In so doing, He explained the power of faith. "Go thy way; thy faith hath made thee whole" (Mark 10:52). You can walk unassisted now, Bartimaeus. You will no longer stumble and fall. Clearly and plainly you will see, for "thy faith hath made thee whole."

The Bible then says, "And immediately he received his sight." No half measures here, but an instantaneous deliverance. Bartimaeus would no longer be referred to as "blind Bartimaeus." For the rest of his life he would tell and retell the miracle of his sight.

The insistence of his cry, in spite of the crowd's rebuke, had been worth it all. He could now see the vivid colors in a butterfly's wings; heretofore, it could only be described to him. He could now delight in the happy smile of a child, and look in wonder at puffy, white clouds in a sky of brilliant blue.

Sunsets were now treasures in gold and red to Bartimaeus. The palm trees, under whose shade he had sat, were now lovely towers of green and yellow. Bartimaeus could see!

But of all these sights, none would ever impress him like the first sight his eyes beheld. For first, he saw the face of Jesus. To be blind and healed; then for your first sight to be that of the Savior must have been quite an experience.

To look into the eyes of mercy, to behold the ears of compassion, to see the lips which spoke words of life, and to gaze upon God's Son's face was a reward of faith Bartimaeus never expected. This glimpse eclipses the healing itself; for in Christ, Bartimaeus embodied complete and total redemption.

The scriptures tell us one more thing about this remarkable man, Bartimaeus. Mark says, "he followed Jesus in the way" (v. 52). There could be no other ending to this story. He is now a follower, a disciple, himself.

How could he not follow the altogether lovely One? This is our lesson. We must follow Him . . . after He heals us of our sin and spiritual blindness.

Amazing grace how sweet the sound
That saved a wretch like me!
I once was lost, but now I'm found,
Was blind, but now, I see."

-John Newton

Bartimeus, the Blind Witness

They came to Jericho: and as he went out of Jericho with his disciples and a great number of people, blind Bartimeus, the son of Timeus, sat by the highway side begging. And when he heard that it was Jesus of Nazareth, he began to cry out, and say, Jesus, thou Son of David, have mercy on me (Mark 10:46, 47).

INTRODUCTION

Jesus Christ came for many reasons; one of those reasons was to heal. Sickness and disease had ravaged the earth since the time of the curse on Adam and Eve. Christ came to destroy the curse. In Nazareth, Jesus quoted Isaiah's prophecy concerning himself and that prophecy said that Messiah would preach the "recovering of sight to the blind."

The story of blind Bartimaeus of Jericho is a story of that prophecy's fulfillment. In this blind man we see character of such depth, he speaks to us from ages past and witnesses that Christ is the healer.

I. JERICHO THE CITY WHERE FOUR BLIND MEN WERE HEALED.

A. Jericho's history and location

Outline

1. City of palm trees, an oasis
2. City of travelers

B. Blindness is prevalent in the hot, sandy, wind-torn Middle East.

   1. One in five are blind or have eye disease.
   2. This was Christ's last trip through Jericho. The time for deliverance was now or perhaps never.

C. The Gospels record four healings of blindness here.

   1. Luke tells of a blind man who was healed "as he was come nigh to Jericho" (Luke 18:35-43).
   2. Matthew tells of two other blind men who were healed as Jesus "departed from Jericho" (Matthew 20:29-34).
   3. Mark tells of Bartimaeus, a blind man who was healed as Jesus "went out of Jericho" (Mark 10:46-52).

II. BARTIMAEUS, A REMARKABLE CHARACTER

A. Though blind, his other senses were keen.

   1. Blind people have to be listeners to survive.
   2. Blind Bartimaeus "heard" Jesus of Nazareth was coming (Mark 10:47).
   3. Bartimaeus reacted immediately, and he began to call on Jesus for mercy (10:47).

B. He was determined and persistent.

   1. Bartimeus would not be quieted by those who wished to silence him (10:48).

Outline

III. JESUS REACTS TO BARTIMAEUS

A. Jesus stood still (10:49).

B. He stopped for a single word.

C. Jesus summoned blind Bartimaeus (10:49) and he came.

D. He tested the blind man's resolve.

   1. Bartimaeus cast aside his garments and went to Jesus (10:50).

   2. His garments represented his past that he was leaving behind.

E. Christ asked him to specify his request (10:51). Here the scripture was demonstrated, "We have not because we ask not."

IV. THE TRIUMPH OF BARTIMAEUS' FAITH

A. His faith was the reason for his healing (10:52).

B. His healing was immediate (10:52).

C. This means that the first thing he ever saw was the face of Jesus. What a reward!

D. He then followed Jesus in the way, meaning he became a disciple (10:52).

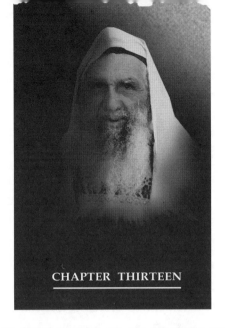

CHAPTER THIRTEEN

STEPHEN
The Faith That Would Not Die

They chose Stephen, a man full of faith and of the Holy Ghost . . . And Stephen, full of faith and power, did great wonders and miracles among the people (Acts 6:5, 8).

THE CHURCH JESUS BEGAN CAME FROM THE UPPER ROOM on the Day of Pentecost filled with world-shaking power. Its growth would be breath-taking and phenomenal. For a world harvest to be reaped, however, the gospel seed would have to be planted in the fertile, blood-soaked ground of martyrdom and sacrifice. Gold must be tried in the fire to prove its purity. Dross is separated from the pristine ore only in the fiery heat of the crucible.

The first of these early Christian martyrs was an extraordinary servant of the Lord named Stephen. He died a horrible and violent death for the cause of Christ. He was a man of God remarkably gifted by the Holy Spirit with spiritual graces and wonderful gifts. His life had earned the confidence of the people and inflamed the bitter enemies of the Cross.

The world he lived in was not worthy of Stephen. His death was indelibly imprinted on the mind of a young Jew named Saul of Tarsus, who witnessed the horrible deed. Saul would sow and reap the harvest that Stephen longed to plant and for which he was willing to give his life.

One cannot study the life of Stephen without feeling genuine humility. There is almost a sense of unworthiness that fills the heart as you read his story.

It is as if you are witnessing something devout and holy. You want to tread lightly as an observer and whisper your thanks to God that such a man existed. You wonder what you would have done in Stephen's place. The inner feelings that plague all true Christians rise at the reading of Stephen's story, and an uncertainty that asks the question, "Could I do likewise?"

STEPHEN'S CHARACTER

The first thing we notice about Stephen is the description the Bible gives of him. He was chosen, along with six other men, by the 12 apostles to conduct the business of the early church in distributing goods and foodstuffs to the poor and needy.

Three qualifications were required for the men chosen: they had to be of honest report, full of the Holy Ghost and filled with wisdom (see Acts 6:3). Each quality is a powerful attribute in the life of any man. But to require all three called for special people indeed.

Seven such men were found. The scriptures list them as Stephen, Philip, Prochorus, Nicanor, Timon, Parmenas and Nicholas (v. 5). Once they were chosen, the apostles laid their hands on them and prayed for God's blessing upon their new endeavors (v. 6).

Of the seven, only two are ever mentioned in Scripture again, although this is not to imply that the other five had lesser roles or did not contribute significantly.

John supposed that if all Jesus himself had said and done was recorded, the world itself could not contain the books (John 21:25). So we know that only some of the exploits of Stephen and Philip are dealt with in scripture.

At the initial selection of these men, it is evident that Stephen was going to be a special vessel of the Lord. While the other six are simply listed, Stephen is said to be "full of faith and of the Holy Ghost" (Acts 6:5). That the writer of Acts would point this out at the listing of the seven deacons is an indication of Stephen's spiritual stature in the early church.

He is described as being "full of faith." Christ had said that faith the size of a grain of mustard seed could move mountains, but here is a man "full of faith." If without faith it is impossible to please God (Hebrews 11:6), then Stephen must have been very pleasing to God.

This kind of faith indicated a heart wholly belonging to God. Stephen was a "sold-out" man.

In addition, this giant of faith was also full of the Holy Ghost. Four times the Bible states that Stephen had this measure of Holy Spirit power (Acts 6:3; 6:5; 6:8; 7:55). It must have been a noticeable characteristic in his life.

Such a man would have to be led of the Holy Spirit. Therefore, the Bible would include Stephen among those sons of God who are led by the Spirit (Romans 8:14). Such a man would know how to wield the Sword of the Spirit, which is the Word of God (see Ephesians 6:17). Stephen did this with uncanny skill and ability in Acts 7.

A man full of the Spirit is a man living holy, because walking in the Spirit forbids him to fulfill the lusts of his flesh (see Galatians 5:16). Stephen was a man of God living a spirit-filled life.

STEPHEN'S ANOINTING

Stephen's faith and spiritual anointing were not in him just to make his own life an acceptable vessel to God. His faith and his power with God were active; and he can be found in Acts 6:8 doing exploits for God in the early days of the church:

> Stephen, full of faith and power, did great wonders and miracles among the people (Acts 6:8).

Jesus said that His followers would have signs following them (Mark 16:17), and Stephen's life was living proof of the validity of that prophecy. Things happen in the ministry of anointed believers.

In those days, "the number of disciples was multiplied" (Acts 6:1). A mighty revival empowered the infant church, and converts to the teachings of Jesus increased rapidly.

The hunger for truth, long suppressed by false religious ideology and the traditions of men, was now being fed with anointed preaching and the demonstration of God's Spirit and power.

But such change always brings dissent. The stubbornness of hardened hearts who refuse the truth will rise up in carnal anger.

Satan has always hated the truth. A few days earlier, he had filled the hearts of Ananias and Sapphira and caused them to lie to the Holy Ghost, resulting in their judgement and instant death (see Acts 5:1-11). Now the preaching and miracles of Stephen and the other apostles would incite Satan's hoodlums to wreak havoc upon the church.

STEPHEN'S PERSECUTION

In this story, we see Satan's deceived henchman useing tactics characteristic of the satanic nature. A number of Jews—principally from the North African regions of Libertina, Cyrene and Alexandria, along with their cohorts from Cilicia and Asia—began to dispute and debate with Stephen (6:9).

In Stephen, however, they found a wise and skilled scholar of the Word. Using that Word and operating in the Holy Spirit within him, he left the would-be debaters in disarray. The scripture states, "They were not able to resist the wisdom and the spirit by which he spake" (v. 6:10).

The Word of God in an anointed servant of the Lord is always irresistible. It destroys the clever mythologies of men, "piercing even to the dividing asunder of soul and spirit, and of the joints and marrow, and is a discerner of the thoughts and the intents of the heart" (Hebrews 4:12).

Jeremiah likened the Word to "a hammer that breaketh the rock in pieces" (Jeremiah 23:29).

Stephen used the wisdom of the Word and his detractors were helpless. Men so possessed of the wicked One are persistent, however. But God was not finished with His servant, Stephen.

These men found false witnesses to testify against Stephen before the Jewish council.

Jezebel had used the same tactic when she found "men of Belial" to lie against Naboth in order to steal his vineyard (see 1 Kings 21:8-10). Since the devil is a liar and the father of lies, he always has children like these ready to do his bidding.

These men lied about Stephen, accusing him of blasphemy and subverting the Law of Moses. They took the prophecies of Jesus concerning the temple that Stephen had preached, and used these to portray Stephen as an insurrectionist who wanted the Jewish way of life destroyed (see Matthew 24:2).

False accusations against such a devout man would wound him to the heart, but Stephen is a choice vessel of God filled with divine purpose. The

Bible lets us see him at the moment these accusations were delivered, and the portrait is one of the most profound in scripture.

> And all that sat in the council, looking steadfastly on him, saw his face as it had been the face of an angel (Acts 6:15).

God allowed His glory to shine through Stephen's face as proof that he was not only telling the truth, but that he was a real man of God. No one present that day would ever forget the glory of God upon Stephen's face.

Angels reveal such reflected glory, but few men have experienced it.

Moses' face glowed with God's glory when he came down from the mount; it had to be covered with a veil (Exodus 34:35). Moses had received the Law on tablets of stone. Now Stephen was preaching of the law having been fulfilled in Christ and written on the believers' hearts. Stephen's face shone likewise.

To the credit of the High Priest, he did give Stephen a chance to respond to these accusations (Acts 7:1). Stephen's defense is one of the greatest discourses found in Holy Writ. It is a composite history of God's dealings with Israel and mankind.

Its sole intent was showing that all things happened as a result of Divine Sovereignty, and that God's plan was to send Jesus as the Messiah.

STEPHEN'S DEFENSE

Stephen dealt first with the Abrahamic Covenant and the establishing of the nation of Israel through Isaac and Jacob (vv. 1-8). He demonstrated to the Jews that God had a purpose for the nation of Israel in the plan of world redemption.

He told the story of Joseph and how God allowed Israel to settle in Egypt always under divine care (vv. 9-16). Then he told the story of Pharaoh's enslavement of Israel and how God raised up Moses through the many twists and turns in his life (vv. 17-34).

This first Christian martyr then painted a portrait of Israel in constant rebellion against God, from their wanderings in the wilderness, through the days of the judges and the time of the kings, until the time he spoke. He told how they worshiped idols, stoned prophets and rejected God's truth over and over.

He mentions their worship of Moloch, an Ammonite god, whose image was a hollow brazen figure filled with hot coals. Little children were placed in its arms and slowly roasted to death (see

Leviticus 18:21; Deuteronomy 18:10; 2 Kings 16:3; Jeremiah 19:5).

To prevent the parents from hearing these dying children's cries, the wicked priests would beat their drums loudly. Such was Israel's disobedience against God for centuries.

In verses 47-50, Stephen recalled that Solomon built them a temple, but pointed out that God doesn't dwell in temples made with hands. He quoted Isaiah 66:1, 2, telling them that God declares, "Heaven is my throne and the earth is my footstool."

His final words are stiff with rebuke and cut like a knife through their hardened hearts. He called them "stiffnecked" (Acts 7:51) using the Greek word *sklerotrachelos*, which portrays the idea of a stubborn ox that cannot be broken; and a neck so strong the animal is useless, because it cannot be turned right or left.

Stephen referred to the people as "uncircumcised in heart," meaning they do not have a covenant relationship of the heart with God — and this is the only thing He will accept.

Stephen accused them of resisting the Holy Ghost as their fathers did. The Greek word here is *antipipto*, which means "to pull against," like a heifer that pulls backward against a rope and will not be led anywhere. In v. 52, he tells them they are the "betrayers and murderers" of the "Just One," meaning Jesus, and they have not even kept the law they received in the first place.

Stephen spoke only three more sentences. His discourse of profound truth had so enraged the demonically-driven mob that they are described by the Acts narrator as being "cut to the heart" (v. 54).

They began to do something only those in a frenzied fit of passionate hatred could do: they gnashed on him with their teeth. Such base and lewd characters these are. Only wild animals in a frothy feeding frenzy could be capable of more than this crowd was capable of.

STEPHEN'S MARTYRDOM

In this moment of incomprehensible behavior, Stephen again shines forth.

> But he, being full of the Holy Ghost, looked up steadfastly into heaven, and saw the glory of God, and Jesus standing on the right hand of God, And said, Behold, I see the heavens opened, and the Son of man standing on the right hand of God (vv. 55, 56).

What testimony from a man who is about to enter the violent crucible of death! What a vision to give hope for all people of the future! In Stephen's critical moment, God in His glory was alive and well and on the throne of His majesty.

Jesus, of whom Stephen had just preached, was at God's right hand. Intercession for the supplicant was taking place. Events on earth did not alter the status of heaven. God could still arise and his enemies must scatter (Psalm 68:1).

God had a purpose in giving this vision to Stephen. He was saying, "My child all is well, I am here."

Assurance, like a warm blanket to a cold child, must have filled Stephen's heart. The air around him was filled with vile cursing and accusations, but his reward was glowing in the glory of God's presence.

At this moment, the crowd around Stephen went berserk with anger. They screamed like banshees and stopped up their ears with their grimy fingers (see Acts 7:57).

They ran at him and dragged him past the gates of the city, gathering up the heavy, jagged stones that cover the hills around Jerusalem. To improve agility, they disrobed and laid their garments at the feet of a young man named Saul.

What impact this may have had on his life we may never know. Yet, we know that many years after this event, the great apostle Paul must have felt an indebtedness for he spent the rest of his life spreading the gospel they died for.

Outside the city, they began to execute Stephen with crude missiles of death. They did it as he was "calling upon God, and saying, Lord Jesus, receive my spirit" (v. 59).

Here is a prayer of confidence prayed in what, for many, would have been a time of great despair. But great faith overcomes great despair. Faith's arms were enfolded around Stephen at death, and his vision of heaven's throne comforted his heart.

The last thing Stephen said was a prayer: "And he kneeled down, and cried with a loud voice, Lord, lay not this sin to their charge. And when he had said this, he fell asleep" (v. 60).

Only Jesus, covered with the blood of Golgotha, had ever uttered such a prayer before (see Luke 23:34). Like his Master, Stephen loved even his executioners.

The love of God in a good person's heart is not extinguished by the hatred and persecution of others. Love grows in the bloody soil of martyrdom. It always thrives when sin and wickedness abound.

Stephen died praying for the lost . . . with a pure heart free from vengeance. Death cannot kill such faith. Such faith will not be destroyed by the loss of breath and the cessation of blood flow.

Twenty centuries later, the testimony of this good man is stronger than ever. Stephen lives on.

When I draw this fleeting breath,
When mine eyes shall close in death,
When I rise to worlds unknown,
And behold Thee on Thy throne,
Rock of Ages, cleft for me,
Let me hide myself in Thee.

-Augustus M. Toplady

Stephen, the Faith That Would Not Die

They chose Stephen, a man full of faith and of the Holy Ghost . . . and Stephen, full of faith and power, did great wonders and miracles among the people (Acts 6:5, 8).

INTRODUCTION

FROM THE DAY OF PENTECOST, THE EARLY CHURCH that Jesus sent forth was filled with world-shaking power. Its growth was breathtaking and phenomenal. Before the world harvest could be reaped, however, the church had to plant the gospel seed in the fertile, blood-soaked ground of martyrdom and sacrifice.

The first of the early Christian martyrs was an extraordinary servant of the Lord named Stephen who died a horrible and violent death for the cause of Christ. The world in which he lived was not worthy of Stephen, but the Christ he proclaimed and the faith he lived would never die. Here is a story of real faith.

I. WHAT KIND OF MAN WAS STEPHEN?

A. He was chosen (*Acts 6:5*).

B. He was to help administrate the business in the infant church.

Outline

C. He was honest and wise (*Acts 6:3*).

D. He was full of faith and power (*Acts 6:8*).

E. He was full of the Holy Ghost (*Acts 6:6*).

II. STEPHEN'S FAITH WAS AN ACTIVE FAITH.

A. He did great wonders and miracles among the people (*Acts 6:8*).

B. His ministry was a fulfillment of Christ's prophecy concerning those who believe (*Mark 16:17*).

III. STEPHEN'S FAITH WAS A FAITH UNDER SIEGE.

A. False religion finds fault with true religion (*Acts 6:9*).

B. Stephen's knowledge of the Word confounded his accusers (*Acts 6:10*).

C. The Word is a powerful weapon against falsehood (*Jeremiah 23:29*).

D. Satan used "liars" and "men of Belial" against Stephen, a tactic he still uses often (*1 Kings 21:8-10*).

E. The glory of God shone through in Stephen's life, even when he was under attack (*Acts 6:15*).

IV. STEPHEN'S DEFENSE OF THE FAITH

A. His defense was Word based (*Acts 7:2-53*).

B. His defense portrayed a pattern to rebellion (*Acts 7:52*).

C. His defense showed God's plan for man (*Acts 7:2*).

D. His defense cut his accusers to the heart (*Acts 7:54*).

Outline

V. STEPHEN DIES IN THE FAITH

A. He died preaching the truth (*Acts 7*).

B. He died with a vision of Christ (*Acts 7:56*).

C. Amazingly, He died praying for forgiveness for his executioners (*Acts 7:60*).

D. He died commending his spirit to God (*Acts 7:59*).

E. His death was much like that of his Master (*Luke 23:46*).

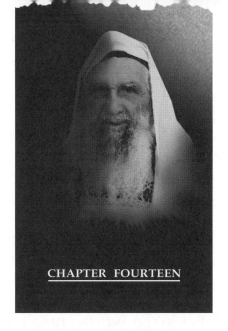

MARY
A Chosen Mother

*And Mary said, My soul doth magnify the Lord, And
my spirit hath rejoiced in God my Saviour. For He hath
regarded the low estate of his handmaiden: for, behold,
from henceforth all generations shall call me blessed*
(Luke 1:46-48).

MARY, MOTHER OF JESUS, is perhaps one of the most
misunderstood people found in Scripture. Some
seek to deify her, adding to her life virtues, graces
and miracles that are not recorded in the Bible.
Others, reacting to this attempt at deification,
ignore her or place her in a role of total
unimportance.

A realistic look at her in scripture reveals a godly woman who never sought for anyone to worship or exalt her. Rather, she tried with all her heart to please God; she took seriously her role as a mother, both to Jesus and to the rest of her children.

MARY AND HER BACKGROUND

The story of Mary is the story of a righteous, peasant girl in an obscure Judean village of Galilee who found favor in the eyes of Him that notices the fall of every sparrow. The omniscient God of eternity knew that the important qualities in her character will be exercised in the nurture and growth of His only begotten son.

Physically, she provided the body and blood for the development of the infant Jesus. Through her He received the life of the flesh—after the Holy Ghost has overshadowed her and the miracle of conception has taken place.

She nursed Him, clothed and fed Him, and provided the intimate care a mother must give a helpless child.

She was a member of the tribe of Judah and came from the house of David, passing her lineage to her Son. Mary was not divine, but was chosen from all women by God Himself; and that makes Mary special, indeed. To exalt her beyond her humanity detracts from the humanness of Jesus and lessens the beauty and power of the Incarnation. To ignore her and her place in the history of God's Son is a historical error at best and a historical crime at worst.

Mary, simply put, is a special, chosen mother. Her story is a story for the ages.

Mary was from the hill village of Nazareth in the land of Galilee. Nazareth sat on a high hill with sheer cliffs that were just outside the gates of the city. It was remote and rural, a village where life had changed little in centuries.

Like most ancient towns of that time, it was virtually self-sustaining, with crops of wheat, corn, olives and grapes growing in the surrounding countryside. Water came from deep wells. The people knew the seasons and how to prepare for lean times and times of plenty.

Various tradesmen plied their trades in Nazareth, catering to the needs of the people. Carpenters, stonemasons, blacksmiths, tanners, weavers, diemakers and many others worked here. They joined with small-time merchants and shopkeepers to keep the cycle of village life intact and provide needed goods and services for the people.

Life in a Judean village was compact and contained, and these hamlets watched the changing governments and rulers over them with a certain disdain and a sense of fatalism. The area of their lives that could not be controlled, however, was their faith in the one true God.

To many, religion had become a system of laws and traditions. Among the peasants, whose lives were a struggle for meager existence, the hope of a better world and a Messiah sent from Jehovah never died.

Every Jewish child knew the stories of Moses, Joshua, Gideon and David, along with the heroes of tradition, such as Judith, Tobit and the Maccabees. There was a pride among these rural people that time and enslavement to the endless taxations of Rome could not erase.

The miracles wrought in the Old Testament were constantly before them; their devotion to their synagogues and the teaching of the rabbis united them in spirit.

A chink appeared in this religious armor, however; and it had to do with the various religious factions which developed in Judaism, causing rifts in the solidarity of the people. Pharisees, Saducees and other groups splintered off on religious tangents, dividing the thinking of the people.

Groups like the Essenes colonized in monasteries and communes. Judaism in the days of Jesus had become somewhat fractured. Still, a righteous remnant remained and looked for the hope and consolation of Israel, which would come through the Messiah.

Into such a world and in such a time, God in wisdom sent His Son. The event itself required a woman to give birth to God in the flesh; and God found her in the tiny, mountain hamlet called Nazareth.

MARY AND GABRIEL

Luke's Gospel gives a detailed account of God's encounter with Mary and the conception of Christ. Matthew adds a commentary that completes the story with grace and finality.

Luke says that the angel Gabriel was sent to Nazareth to announce a never-has-happened-before event to Mary (1:26, 27). Luke calls her "a virgin," using the Greek word *pauthenos*, which means "a pure virgin woman who has never had a sexual relationship with a man."

Literally, she had never engaged in the physical act of copulation. Isaiah's prophecy concerning the virgin birth of the Messiah in Isaiah 7:14 uses the Hebrew word *almah*, which has the same basic meaning.

Mary, Luke tells us, was "espoused to a man whose name was Joseph" (Luke 1:27). He was a carpenter in Nazareth.

———

Espousal was the legal written marriage agreement among the Hebrews. It was a contract, a legal document, signed by all parties involved. It specified the length of time between the espousal and the actual marriage ceremony, and—this is important—between the marriage and the conjugal relationship. This agreement could only be dissolved by a bill of divorcement.

Joseph, at this time, could have been 30 years of age or even older. Most likely Mary was in her upper teen years, or perhaps had turned 20. Their ages are speculation based on Jewish customs and traditions of the time, but those with knowledge of the times place them, most likely, at about this age.

Gabriel visited Mary, and their conversation is worthy of commentary. Gabriel told her she was "highly favored, the Lord is with thee: blessed art thou among women" (Luke 1:28).

The word *favored* here is found only twice in the New Testament (Luke 1:28; Ephesians 1:6). It means "endued with grace." Grace, of course, is God's unmerited favor. The message here means that Mary was the recipient of God's great grace and goodness.

A visit by an angel would be troubling, even in our media-oriented society. But to a poor peasant girl, it was very disturbing. "She was troubled at his saying, and cast in her mind what manner of salutation this should be" (Luke 1:29).

The Greek word used is *diatarasso* which means "to be very disturbed," as opposed to being slightly troubled. This was the reason for Gabriel's words of comfort, "fear not," in verse 30.

The great messenger angel then informed her that she would conceive in her womb and bear a son. She was to call His name Jesus.

"Jesus" is the Greek form of the Hebrew *Yehoshua* or Joshua, and is found 979 times in the New Testament. It literally means "Savior" or "God who is Salvation."

The description Gabriel gives of Him leaves no doubt that the One he speaks of is Israel's intended Messiah.

> He shall be great, and shall be called the Son of the Highest: and the Lord God shall give unto him the throne of his father David: And he shall reign over the house of Jacob forever; and of his kingdom there shall be no end (vv. 32, 33).

Mary, either through lack of knowledge of Isaiah's prophecy (Isaiah 7:14) or because of the overwhelming excitement of the moment, asked the question, "How shall this be, seeing I know not a man?" (v. 34). Like all human beings, she understood the physical requirements for conception to take place.

Gabriel explained the process that would take place in order for this to be a virgin birth:

> The Holy Ghost shall come upon thee, and the power of the Highest shall overshadow thee: therefore also that holy thing which shall be born of thee shall be called the Son of God (vv. 35).

Then Gabriel told Mary that her aged and barren cousin, Elisabeth, was six months pregnant with John the Baptist, and added that "with God nothing shall be impossible" (v. 37). Mary then surrendered herself as "the handmaid of the Lord" (v. 38) and asked for God's will to be done in her life.

Mary went "with haste" (v. 39) to visit Elisabeth. More than likely, this was a visit of both confirmation and spiritual necessity.

Mary told Elisabeth the glorious story of Gabriel's salutation, and the unborn babe leaped in Elisabeth's womb. The Holy Ghost filled Elisabeth. Without hesitation, Elisabeth acknowledged Mary to be "the mother of my Lord" (v. 43).

What faith this elderly Hebrew mother had! She told Mary that when she heard the glad news, her "babe leaped in my womb for joy" (v. 44).

These events were foreshadowing John and his ministry as the forerunner of Christ. Elisabeth then prophesied that God would do all the things He had told Mary (v. 45). Mary must have had great confidence in Elisabeth's godly life.

Godly women tend to trust each other and depend on each other for affirmation in spiritual matters. Their suppressed role in history by a male-dominated society often draws them together in a spiritual bond, because they understand the nature and personality of the female gender.

Elisabeth believed Mary, and Mary believed Elisabeth. Mary's prayer of rejoicing, called "The Magnificat," is a portrait of a woman enraptured in praise to God. In verse 47, she calls God, "God my Savior."

This certainly dispels the teaching that Mary had no sinful nature or was sinless herself. She acknowledged that she had, and needed, a Savior. She glorified God and spoke of His ability to humble the mighty and exalt the lowly. She gave praise to Him for remembering Israel and Abraham's seed (vv. 51-55).

Mary stayed with Elisabeth for three months until the birth of John, no doubt assisting her in her last months of pregnancy, before returning to Nazareth.

Matthew gives further insight into what must have been one of the most difficult times of Mary's life. To be with child is to change the shape of a woman's body and the secret cannot be kept forever.

Tiny villages have no secrets and soon everyone in Nazareth would know of Mary's condition. Horror of horrors, Joseph would know! Mary most likely told him, but Joseph was human enough to have doubts. After all, since Adam there had been no virgin births on the earth. Physically, it was impossible.

MARY AND JOSEPH

A thousand questions must have bombarded Joseph's troubled mind. He knew he was not the father of the coming Child. Had his betrothed been assaulted? Had she been foolish? What had happened?

Here is a man who deserves our sympathy. It is evident that Joseph truly loved Mary. The Law of Moses allowed her to be put to death by stoning (see Deuteronomy 22:25-28). Joseph would have been within his rights to take her before the Jewish magistrates.

But the Bible tells us that Joseph had pretty well decided that, as soon as he could work out the logistics, he would "put her away privily" (Matthew 1:19).

This means he would have to arrange for a private legal divorce and allow her to go her way unharmed. His heart was likely broken and his dreams of a future with Mary shattered.

At this point we are shown that God had chosen not only Mary, but Joseph as well. He, too, was to parent and raise His Son. The angel Gabriel makes the first of several visits to Joseph. In Matthew 1:20, 21, he is told by the angel:

> Fear not to take unto thee Mary thy wife: for that which is conceived in her is of the Holy Ghost. And she shall bring forth a son, and thou shalt call his name Jesus: for he shall save his people from their sins." When he awoke, Joseph demonstrated remarkable faith and immediately married Mary (v. 24).

The last verse of Matthew 1 tells us two things about this young couple from Nazareth. The Bible says that Joseph "knew her not until she had brought forth her firstborn son" (Matthew 1:25). They did not have a physical marriage relationship until after Christ's birth.

But the word "until" indicates that a normal marriage relationship existed thereafter. Mary and Joseph had other natural-born children. Jesus had at least four half-brothers—James, Joses, Simon, and Judas—and several sisters (see Matthew 13:55, 56; Mark 6:3; Luke 8:19-21). False claims of Mary's perpetual virginity contradict Holy Scripture.

Mary and Joseph loved each other and stood by each other in the most difficult of times.

Two of Jesus' brothers became great apostles and early church leaders, giving us the powerful books of James and Jude.

To understand Mary as a mother, you must understand her relationship with all her children, and the difficulties it must have involved knowing the eldest was the Son of God.

Considering the natural occurrence of sibling rivalries, the whole scenario leaves us with a thousand unanswered questions; but God trusted Mary, and she must have handled it quite well.

MARY AND BABY JESUS

Her beautiful example during the event-filled days of His birth and infancy is noteworthy. Just before Jesus' birth, Luke tells of Mary and Joseph's journey from Nazareth to Bethlehem to be taxed and to participate in a Roman census (see Luke 2). Bethlehem, just south of Jerusalem, was David's home city and since Joseph was of the house of David, he was required to go there for this legal obligation.

The first night in the city found the young couple without a place to stay, because of the overcrowding caused by the census. Mary's labor pains began and they found shelter in an animal stable. There Mary gave birth to the Son of God.

The Greek word used for the manger in which the new-born Baby was laid is *phathe*, which means "an animal crib" or "feeding place." Jesus was wrapped in "swaddling clothes," which are like bandages, and laid in a manger.

(Their custom involved wrapping newborn babies in cloth, like a mummy with no sign of the arms or legs. A baby's social status and rank in life were determined by the costliness of the garments. Rich children of status were wrapped in silks and fine linen, while the poor used homespun or less costly garments. The practice is mentioned in Job 38:9.)

That night the angels sang of His glory. Shepherds told of the angelic choir and went to see this Babe in the manger. The Bible points out that "Mary kept all these things and pondered them in her heart" (Luke 2:19).

One wonders what this young Hebrew mother must have felt, holding this special child to her breast. She had delivered Him in birth and He would deliver her from sin. She held in her arms God's love to the world. Yet, as a human baby, He needed her love and care so desperately. The next few days of Jesus' life were remarkable.

✓ Simeon and Anna gave their prophecies of Him at His circumcision on the eighth day of His life (2:21-38).

✓ Three Kings from the east sought out this newborn King of Kings and brought Him expensive gifts of gold, frankincense and myrrh (Matthew 2:11).

✓ Joseph was warned by an angel of God concerning Herod's death sentence on infants, and took Mary and her little son to Egypt until it was safe to return to Judea (vv. 13-23).

All of these events were signs of confirmation to Mary that indeed, God was doing a marvelous thing on the earth. She handled her role with dignity and devotion.

Luke shows us Jesus at the age of 12. His parents went to the Passover in Jerusalem every year, indicating their religious devotion and the training through example they were giving to their children. They traveled with large family groups, and all indications are that it was a festive occasion and a time of reunion.

After a full day's journey out of Jerusalem on the way back home, the parents discovered that Jesus was missing.

The Bible indicates this was not neglect on their part, but rather an assumption that He was with their other kinsfolk and friends (see Luke 2:44). They searched frantically for Him, returning to Jerusalem and looking for three full days before finding Him in the temple.

One can imagine their fear and consternation, for these were days of slavery, and Romans thought nothing of capturing their young subjects and forcing them to their bidding.

Jesus, however, was found in the Temple, involved in deep theological discussions with learned doctors "both hearing them, and asking them questions (v. 46). The Bible says, "And all that heard him were astonished at his understanding and answers (v. 47).

Questioning Jesus about His disappearance, Mary told Him of her and Joseph's fright and worry. His response is Jesus' first recorded words in the Gospels: "How is it that ye sought me? wist ye not that I must be about my Father's business?" (v. 29).

Jesus was saying, "Why are you worried, I am doing what my Father revealed to you by the angels that I came to do." Still, the Bible records, "They understood not" (v. 50).

Although Jesus was the Son of God, He was subject to His parents. He returned with them to Nazareth.

The Biblical record of the rest of His childhood is simply, "And Jesus increased in wisdom and stature, and in favor with God and man" (v. 52).

MARY AND THE ADULT JESUS

No one really knows all that Mary went through as Jesus grew, developed and began His ministry. We are given glimpses of Mary throughout the New Testament. The most extended portraits of her are found, however, at His birth, during His childhood and at the traumatic scene of His death.

She was present for His first miracle at Cana in Galilee (John 2:1-11), when He turned water into wine at a wedding. At the tiny town of Cana, near Nazareth, she was most likely either related to the wedding party or a close friend of the family.

She took it on herself to correct the matter of the wine being gone. The Bible says that Jesus and His disciples were there (John 2:2). Mary implored Jesus to do something about the problem of no wine. Jesus told her respectfully that the time of the revelation of His ministry had not come yet.

Then Mary made a bold statement of faith. She told the servants, "Whatsoever he saith unto you, do it" (v. 5). I believe that Jesus, out of pure love for His mother, came to her rescue in a moment of social and religious embarrassment.

He performed the miracle and turned water into excellent wine. The wedding feast was a success and the miracle ministry of Jesus had begun. We have no written record of this, but I believe that Mary smiled! Then she is seen in Galilee with His other siblings, searching for Jesus and unable to reach Him for the multitudes (Luke 8:19-21).

Mary watched Jesus die for the sins of the world. She probably knew for a long time that it was going to happen. I believe that after He had been her son for 33 years, she understood the plan of redemption. If she did, she knew she would have to give Him up.

What prepares a mother for something like this? Nothing can soften the blow of the death of a child. The horror of His lacerated and bleeding body, racked with pain and the shame of nakedness, only increased her consternation.

Only a mother could look at Him dying and see the newborn babe, the waddling toddler, the bright-eyed, tree-climbing little boy, and the changing teenager.

Mary must have remembered His favorite dishes. She often re-lived His times with her alone, and the warmth of His embrace.

She is not seen at the Resurrection, and this raises many questions concerning her whereabouts. They can probably be answered by understanding her profound grief. The danger to her person from the Jews was real, and perhaps, because of her age, the sheer physical strain of his death had weakened her.

When He died He saw her, too. In His suffering He told His beloved disciple, John, to take care of her (John 19:25-27). They loved each other to the very end, this Son of God and His Galilean mother. He died and her heart broke. He arose and her heart must have leaped!

On the day of Pentecost, 10 days after the Ascension, the Holy Spirit fell in an Upper Room in Jerusalem. Mary was present in the Upper Room with her other sons on the day of Pentecost. They received the outpouring of the Holy Spirit (see Acts 1:14)

Peter, James, John and all the rest of the 120 disciples felt the power of the Holy Ghost for the first time.

Not Mary! She recognized His presence.

Years before, the same Spirit had overshadowed her, a young peasant girl, and she became a chosen mother.

Silent Night, Holy Night,
All is calm, All is bright,
Round yon virgin, Mother and Child
Holy Infant so tender and mild,
Sleep in Heavenly Peace,
Sleep in Heavenly Peace.

-Joseph Mohr

Mary, a Chosen Mother

And Mary said, My soul doth magnify the Lord, And my spirit hath rejoiced in God my Savior. For He hath regarded the low estate of his handmaiden: for, behold, from henceforth all generations shall call me blessed (Luke 1:46-48).

INTRODUCTION

Mary, the mother of Jesus, is perhaps one of the most misunderstood people found in scripture. Some seek to deify her and add to her life virtues, graces and miracles that never occurred according to the Bible.

Others, as a reaction to this attempt at deification, ignore her or place her in a role of total unimportance. The truth is, Mary was chosen by God to be the mother of His Son. She must have been, in fact she had to be, a very special lady indeed. Hers is a story for the ages.

I. MARY AND HER SIMPLE BACKGROUND

A. Nazareth is a Galilean hill village.

B. Life was rural and agrarian in nature.

C. The people's faith in Jehovah had endured, despite national dominance by Rome and the religious fragmenting of Judaism.

Outline

D. A righteous remnant in Israel awaited the Messiah.

E. Mary was an espoused virgin.

 1. She had never "known" a man (*Luke 1:34*).

 2. She and a carpenter, named Joseph, had signed an espousal contract but had not yet married (*Luke 1:27*).

II. MARY AND THE ANGEL GABRIEL

A. God "highly favored" Mary (*Luke 1:28*).

B. She was told of the coming conception of Christ within her (*Luke 1:31*).

C. She was given a verbal portrait painting her Son as the obvious Messiah (*Acts 1:32-33*).

D. Mary accepted the will of God in her life (Luke 1:38).

III. MARY AND JOSEPH'S PROBABLE STRUGGLE

A. There was no precedent; this had never happened before in history.

B. There were many doubters.

C. Mary's pregnancy before marriage put her in danger, of death, according to the law (*Deuteronomy 22:25-28*).

D. Joseph, a kind and just man, decided to divorce her privately, allowing her to live.

E. Joseph was also a chosen vessel, and he accepted Mary's innocence when God confirmed it to him (*Matthew 1:20, 21*).

Outline

IV. MARY AND CHRIST'S CHILDHOOD

A. Jesus' birth and the circumstances surrounding it (*Matthew 2:1-18; Luke 2:1-20*)

B. His circumcision in the temple (*Luke 2:21-39*)

C. His disappearance at age 12 (*Luke 2:40-52*)

D. The Biblical fact of His siblings — the other children of Mary and Joseph (*Matthew 13:55, 56; Mark 6:3; Luke 8:19-21*)

V. MARY AND THE ADULT JESUS

A. She was at His first miracle at Cana (*John 2:1-11*).

B. She was at His death on Calvary and heard Him ask John to care for her (*John 19:26-33*).

C. She was with the 120 believers, along with her other sons, on the day of Pentecost (*Acts 1:14*).

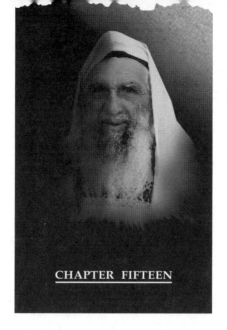

BARNABAS
Son of Consolation

Then tidings of these things came unto the ears of
the church which was in Jerusalem: and they sent forth
Barnabas, that he should go as far as Antioch. . . . For
he was a good man, and full of the Holy Ghost and of faith:
and much people was added unto the Lord
(Acts 11:22, 24).

AS IN LIFE, OFTEN IN SCRIPTURE SOME OF THE MEN AND WOMEN seem to overshadow the more prominent heroes and heroines in the Bible.

Their deeds are not as flamboyant, and they are willing to be subservient to more outgoing and vocal personalities. They are usually seen doing the menial tasks in the everyday, pragmatic business of

God's Kingdom. Their good works often go unnoticed, even when recorded in Holy Writ.

This does not lessen their stature in the eyes of the all-seeing God of eternity, however. He who judges men's deeds and sees their hearts will reward His own accordingly. After all, "the Lord knoweth them that are His" (2 Timothy 2:19).

MAN OF MANY VIRTUES

Barnabas was such a man. Trustworthy and dependable as well as honest and patient, he embodied virtues that the early church desperately needed as it grew and developed.

People like Barnabas are also urgently needed in this hour — men and women who long to fulfill the role of a true servant.

Comforting Consoler

According to Acts 4:36, Barnabas' name means "son of consolation." To console is to comfort and bolster. Consolation is reinforcement given by the strong to those who are weakened by the cares of life.

Barnabas' name was a true label of the man. His first introduction in scriptures shows him giving a large sum of money to the church in Jerusalem. The money came from the sale of a parcel of land (v. 37).

Generous Giver

No fanfare accompanied this act of giving. He simply takes the entire sale price and lays it at the feet of the apostles. The first virtue we see in Barnabas, then, is the grace of generosity.

He was a giving man. Since God gave His Son; and Jesus, God's Son, gave His life; it is easily concluded that giving is part of the nature of God. This godly quality was evident in the life of Barnabas.

He was not a Christian in words only; he actively participated in living out the principles of Christ.

Ministering Levite

Barnabas was a Levite (v. 36). This means he descended from that tribe in Israel to whom the duties of the priesthood had been assigned. There can be no doubt that he had a background in the oracles of the laws of God. His foundational structure was the Word of God, and this served him well as a servant of the Lord in the days of the early church.

This first-century church leader took an early interest in the life of Saul of Tarsus, the man who was to become the great apostle Paul. After Paul's conversion and baptism in the Holy Ghost, he preached Christ in the synagogues of Damascus. He then went to Arabia for three years (see Galatians 1:17).

On returning to Jerusalem he sought out the apostles, but those early disciples were afraid of him (Acts 9:26). As Saul, he had been such a persecutor of the Christians and such a devoted agent of the high priest that they could not believe he had been, or could be, converted.

Promoter of Others

At this point we see the intervention of Barnabas. He personally presented Saul to the apostles and vouched for the new Christian's character (v. 27). This act may very well be one of the most underrated feats in the entire New Testament.

God used Barnabas in an amazing way, because he had the trust of people. His life was a flawless example of what a Christian should be.

For Barnabas to vouch for Saul was not only an exemplary act of kindness, it opened a door of affiliation for Saul with the New Testament Church, which in turn would become the platform from which he would launch his missionary ministry.

MISSIONARY VISION

One of Barnabas' few solo missions is recorded in chapter 11. Word reached Jerusalem that at Antioch, a number of Greek-speaking Jews had received Christ and "the hand of the Lord was with them" (v. 21). Barnabas was immediately dispatched to Antioch to secure this new work and to instruct them in the ways of the Lord.

When Barnabas arrived at Antioch, his mission took on a four-fold dimension. *He was first of all, an observer of God's grace.* The Bible said he saw "the grace of God" (v. 23). This means he saw the works of, and the results of, God's grace.

Grace is not an invisible virtue. Instead, it is a marvelous thing to observe. Grace is the unmerited favor of God, and when it is in action, lives are dramatically changed. Barnabas saw this working of grace.

The Bible tells of a second dimension of Barnabas' mission: he was glad. Barnabas became emotionally involved in what God was doing at Antioch, and his reaction was happiness.

A true Christian is filled with gladness when he or she sees God's grace in the lives of others. Only the carnal and unregenerate grow jealous, angry or weary at the moving of God in people's lives. Barnabas was glad because of what God had done.

Thirdly, Barnabas began to exhort the people. Exhortation is an admonishment, or an urging to a course of action. This is vocal persuasion of the highest order. This describes what beloved

Barnabas, the son of consolation, gave to the new Christians at Antioch.

The fourth dimension of Barnabas' involvement at Antioch directed his exhortation. He exhorted them to "cleave unto the Lord" with "purpose of heart (see v. 23). What glorious advice! Men and women cleaving to the Lord are not likely to be blown about by every wind and manner of doctrine.

Barnabas' godly demeanor and Christ-like example greatly influenced the new church at Antioch. The Bible says that "much people was added unto the Lord" (v. 24).

Then Barnabas went to Tarsus and found Saul. They both went back to Antioch where they met with the church, teaching and instructing the believers for a whole year.

Their teaching must have been dynamic and life-changing, because here we have one of the great statements in the Bible: "The disciples were called Christians first in Antioch" (11:26). What the world would call God's people until the end of time first got its start in Antioch.

Imagine people so much like Christ that they became known as Christians. Barnabas had much to do with this powerful development. He knew Paul's ability as a teacher, so he took him to

Antioch—even if it meant a lesser role for himself. Here was a man without an ego problem. He wanted results, not recognition. Souls were more important to him than salutations.

God honors such men. When they humble themselves before Him, He exalts them in due time.

PAUL'S HELPER

Famine struck Jerusalem about this time, and the growing church at Antioch raised funds for the relief of the saints in Judea (vv. 27-29). Barnabas and Saul were sent on a relief mission to Jerusalem with these funds.

When they returned to Antioch, they began an intense ministry of prayer and fasting. Such devotion always brings results, and in those days the Holy Ghost spoke plainly in Antioch. The Holy Ghost said,

> Separate me Barnabas and Saul for the work whereunto I have called them (13:2).

The men of Antioch laid hands on these two men and sent them on what would become known as the first great missionary journey. What an itinerary! They traveled first to Seleucia in Syria; then to the island of Cyprus in the Mediterranean Sea, visiting the cities of

Salamis and Paphos. From there they went to the Asia Minor cities of Perga in Pamphylia; and Antioch Pisidia, Iconium, Lystra and Derbe in Iconium.

On the trip back they visited and witnessed in four of the same cities again, picking up Attalia along the way. Then they returned to their home base in Antioch Syria.

During these journeys Saul, now called Paul (see v. 9), began to come to the forefront as the chief speaker and leader of the pair. But Barnabas remained his faithful companion. He was always a steadfast, dependable pillar that Paul could, and did, lean on.

The scriptures are almost totally silent about Barnabas the leader from this moment on, although he is mentioned constantly in conjunction with Paul as their adventures unfold.

This leads us to perhaps the most recognizable of Barnabas' virtues—his genuine humility. Barnabas was a man in love with the Lord, and therefore he was a humble man.

✓ He stood by Paul as Paul defied Elymas the Sorcerer (vv. 8-11).

✓ He was there when they were cast out of Antioch in Pisidia (13:50).

✓ He saw the crippled man healed at Lystra (14:10).

✓ He was mistaken for the god, Jupiter, and Paul was mistaken for Mercury after this miracle. They rebuked the worship of the people, pointing them to Christ (vv. 12-18).

✓ Barnabas thrilled at what the Gospel was doing for the Gentiles and stood firmly with Paul at the Jerusalem Council in Acts 15, defending the truth that the Gospel was for all nations.

UNPOPULAR STAND

An unfortunate incident ends our view of Barnabas in the Book of Acts. It doesn't detract from his character, however; but rather teaches us the lesson that Christians can disagree while maintaining their righteousness and their integrity.

Paul and Barnabas were about to leave on their second missionary journey. They had been a wonderful team, and God had given them great victories.

As they prepared for the journey, Barnabas wanted to take his nephew, Mark (see Colossians 4:10). Paul was against this move, perhaps because Mark had been with them on their first missionary journey and had left before its completion (see Acts 12:25; 13:5,13).

The Bible says, "And the contention was so sharp between them, that they departed asunder one from the other"(15:39). Barnabas took Mark and sailed to Cyprus; Paul chose Silas and they went overland to Asia Minor.

In this dispute, it is safe to say that Paul was pragmatic and practical. He knew the vigors and dangers of missionary work. He did not want to risk taking along a novice who appeared to him to be immature and unprepared for the journey.

Barnabas, however, acted out of love and trust. He wanted to believe in the best of the young man. Both of these New Testament giants were right in their thinking, but their opinions collided.

Rather than wreak havoc on the work of God, they went their separate ways. Paul's opinion of Mark would change dramatically in later years and he would even ask for him to come to him (2 Timothy 4:11).

Mark, a convert of Peter (see 1 Peter 5:13), became the great Gospel writer and contributed much to the early church and to the body of Christ.

Barnabas, the son of consolation, believed in his nephew. Here is an example for all mature adults. Young people need strong, mature Christians to trust them and put faith in them.

Sure, they may fail. A child learning to walk will stumble from time to time, but he or she needs a chance. Barnabas believed in Mark and stood by him. It made a difference.

Standing up for Mark probably cost Barnabas a larger role in recorded history, but it was worth it. God established Paul to be the proclaimer of the gospel to the Gentile world, and another quiet man named Silas began to travel with him.

But one has to admire Barnabas. He believed in a young man who was just learning—just as he had believed in Saul of Tarsus when he was first converted.

We now have Mark's Gospel and Paul's Epistles—probably the end results of a good example for all of us named Barnabas.

When we walk with the Lord
In the Light of His word,
What a glory He sheds on our way!
While we do His good will,
He abides with us still,
And with all who will trust and obey.

Trust and obey, for there's no other way
To be happy in Jesus,
But to trust and obey.

-John H. Sammis

Barnabas, Son of Consolation

Then tidings of these things came unto the ears of the church which was in Jerusalem: and they sent forth Barnabas that he should go as far as Antioch . . . For he was a good man, and full of the Holy Ghost and faith: and much people was added unto the Lord (Acts 11:22, 24)

INTRODUCTION

Often in Scripture, as in life, we find men and women whose roles are overshadowed by the more prominent heroes and heroines in the Bible. Their deeds are not flamboyant and they are willing to be subservient to more outgoing and vocal personalities.

These lesser known people are often found doing menial tasks in the every-day, pragmatic business of God's Kingdom. Their good works often go unnoticed even when recorded in Holy Writ. This, however, does not lessen their stature in the eyes of the all seeing God of eternity.

He who judges men's deeds and sees their hearts will reward every person accordingly. After all "the Lord knoweth them that are His" (2 Timothy 2:19). Barnabas embodied virtues that the early church desperately

Outline

needed as it grew and developed in its infancy. This kind of individual — one who longs to fulfill the role of a true servant — is also needed, urgently, in this hour.

I. BARNABAS WAS A MAN WITH MANY VIRTUES.

A. His name means "son of consolation" (*Acts 4:36*).
B. He was a generous man (*Acts 4:37*).
C. He was a Levite who ministered before the Lord.
D. He promoted others such as Saul (see *Acts 9:27*).

II. BARNABUS WAS A MAN WITH A MISSIONARY VISION.

A. He went to Antioch to establish the church.
   1. He observed what God had done (*Acts 11:23*).
   2. He gave godly exhortations (*Acts 11:23*).
   3. He demonstrated goodness and faith(*Acts 11:24*).
   4. He saw results — "much people was added to the Lord" (*Acts 11:24*).
B. He went back to Antioch and took Saul with him.
   1. They established a Bible training school (*Acts 11:26*).
   2. They sent relief to the famine-ravaged saints in Judea (*Acts 11:29, 30*).
   3. They were called to missionary work (*Acts 13:2*).
   4. The term "Christian" was first used when they were at Antioch (*Acts 11:26*).

Outline

III. BARNABAS BECAME PAUL'S HELPER.

A. He stayed in the background on their first missionary journey. He respected Paul's gift and calling; he was a servant.

B. He stood beside Paul in the Jerusalem Council in Acts 15, affirming with Paul that the gospel was for the Gentiles, too.

IV. BARNABAS TOOK AN UNPOPULAR STAND.

A. Paul and Barnabas had a heated dispute over Mark (*Acts 15:39*).

   1. Paul didn't want Mark on the second missionary journey, for he had abandoned them on the first one (*Acts 12:25; 13:5,13*).

   2. Barnabas, Mark's uncle, loved him and was willing to forgive his mistake.

B. The dispute separated Barnabas and Saul (*Acts 15:39*).

   1. Barnabas' assessment of Mark proved to be correct.

   2. Young people need someone to believe in them (*1 Timothy 4:15*).

C. Mark later would write the great Gospel of Mark.

D. Paul would grow in greatness and Barnabas is not seen any more; but his example of servanthood and crucifixion of self lives on.